Still in STEAM

Jacket: *Torbay & Dartmouth Railway's Prairie tank starting the 1-in-66 climb to Greenway Tunnel.*/Robin Russell

Previous page: *LMS Jubilee 4-6-0 (4) 5593* Kolhapur *at Tyseley in May 1970.*/J. H. Cooper-Smith

Below: *Headed by LSWR 0-4-4T No 24* Calbourne *the first train run by the Isle of Wight Steam Railway leaving Newport Station for Havenstreet in January 1971, four years after closure of the line by BR.*/Gary Merrin

Still in STEAM

E. L. Cornwell

LONDON

IAN ALLAN LTD

Contents

Below: Double headed by J72 0-6-0T No 69023 and KWVR's USA 0-6-0T No 72, a train loaded with NELPG North Eastern Special passengers climbing out of Keighley in June 1969./V. K. C. Allen

Overleaf: National Railway Museum's LNWR No 790 Hardwicke heading a train out of York Layerthorpe for Dunnington, on the Derwent Valley Light Railway, in October 1976. The run was to test the possibility of operating passenger excursions over the privately owned commercial goods only 4-mile DVLR, which were in fact started in 1977./M. Hall

First published 1978

ISBN 0 7110 0850 7

Published by Ian Allan Ltd, Shepperton, Surrey; and printed in the United Kingdom by Ian Allan Printing Ltd

Introduction

This book is a completely new edition of a title first published in 1969. Like its predecessor, it is not intended as an addition to the several existing catalogues of preserved railways and railway vehicles. Its purpose is to provide a broad background to the cult of steam railway preservation in Britain and a guide only to how and where it is practised by its devotees and can be seen and savoured by the interested spectator. *Still in Steam* also provides an opportunity to publish another collection of the excellent pictures that the operation of steam railways has always seemed to generate in greater abundance and variety than any other human pursuit.

How a Steam Locomotive Works

B. K. Cooper

EARLY RAILWAYS provided the ballad-mongers with a new subject. The opening of one line was heralded in a penny song-sheet in the following words:

What a wonderful thing it will be for to see
A long string of carriages on the railway
All loaded with passengers inside and out
And moved by what comes from a tea kettle's spout.

It is a homely image, but one which must have occurred to many when they first saw a locomotive. We hear echoes of it still in comments to the effect that the usefulness of a steam locomotive could be measured by its ability to boil water.

The locomotive boiler (Fig 1) is formed of rings of steel plate which are joined together to form a watertight barrel. At the cab end of the barrel is a separate structure, the firebox. This consists of an outer steel wrapper plate and an inner firebox of copper, with a water space between them. The firebox is an extension of the boiler barrel, and when the boiler is filled the water covers the top and sides of the inner firebox.

The fire grate is at the bottom of the firebox and is fed with coal through a fire door in the cab. Heat from the fire is transmitted through the walls of the inner firebox to the surrounding water. Even if there were no obstructions in the way, the grate could not extend the full length of the boiler because it would be impossible to throw the coal to the far end. But it is important to heat as much of the water as possible directly, and so the heating surface represented by the area of the firebox walls in contact with water must be increased. Additional heating surface is provided by tubes, called fire tubes, which extend through the boiler from the front of the inner firebox to a tubeplate at the other end separating the boiler barrel from the smokebox. Hot gases from the fire flow through the tubes, heating the surrounding water on the way, and pass into the smokebox, from where they escape into the atmosphere through the chimney.

When the engine is working the exhaust steam is also discharged through the chimney and creates a vacuum in the smokebox. The exhaust shoots the smoke and hot gases from the fire forcefully out through the chimney and the vacuum created draws air in over the grate and through the tubes to help combustion of the fuel.

Tables of locomotive dimensions show the exterior area of the firebox and the sum of the exterior areas of all the tubes. Added together they give the total heating surface. Often the steam generated in the boiler is heated further as it flows to the cylinders by means of a superheater, as described later.

When the boiler is filled to its working level there is still space above the water, and it is there that the steam collects. It is desirable to draw the steam off from a point as far as possible above the water level where it will be relatively dry. Extra space is often provided by that familiar and self-explanatory boiler fitting, the dome. It is there that the steam pipe to the

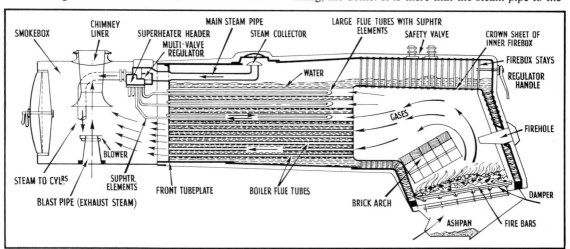

SMOKEBOX — CHIMNEY LINER — SUPERHEATER HEADER — MULTI-VALVE REGULATOR — MAIN STEAM PIPE — STEAM COLLECTOR — LARGE FLUE TUBES WITH SUPHTR. ELEMENTS — SAFETY VALVE — CROWN SHEET OF INNER FIREBOX — FIREBOX STAYS — REGULATOR HANDLE — WATER — FIREHOLE — GASES — STEAM TO CYLRS — BLOWER — SUPHTR. ELEMENTS — FRONT TUBEPLATE — BOILER FLUE TUBES — BRICK ARCH — DAMPER — BLAST PIPE (EXHAUST STEAM) — ASHPAN — FIRE BARS

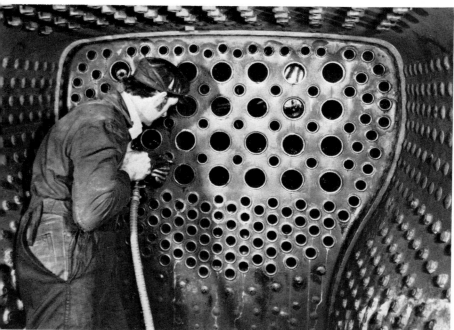

Above: *Assembled boiler of a WD 2-10-0 locomotive ready for the erection shop at North British Locomotive Company's Glasgow works.*

Left: *A major job retubing the boiler of 4-6-0 No 7029* Clun Castle *in 1975 with a Birmingham Railway Museum, Tyseley, boilersmith working inside the firebox./Tubes Ltd*

Above right: *One of the famous LNER Gresley A4 Pacifics, No 2509* Silver Link *getting its boiler lagging in the erecting shop at Doncaster Works in about 1935./Peter Rawson*

engine proper begins, and often the flow of steam is controlled by a regulator valve inside the dome. Alternatively the regulator may be in the smokebox. Some locomotive boilers are domeless, but sufficient space above the water for collecting dry steam is provided by building them with a taper so that the barrel becomes deeper towards the firebox.

The working pressures of boilers range from about 180 to 275lb/sq in. If steam is generated faster than it is being used in the cylinders the pressure could rise above the rated pressure of the boiler. To prevent this a spring-loaded safety-valve is fitted, usually on top of the outer firebox, which opens automatically when the critical pressure is reached. Steam then 'blows off' through the valve until pressure has fallen below the rated value, when the spring closes the valve.

An inclined arch of firebrick or similar material is built across the firebox below the lowest row of tubes so that the hot gases from the fire cannot enter them directly and bypass the upper ones. In curving round the arch the gases spread uniformly to flow through all the tubes. An inclined scoop on the inside of the firebox door has a similar function in directing the incoming air which is necessary for combustion of the fuel, so that it mingles uniformly with the gases. The grate itself consists of firebars at the bottom of the inner firebox with the ashpan below them. Air is also drawn in through the grate and this supply can be regulated by the fireman by means of dampers incorporated in the ashpan.

Steam generated in a boiler by the methods described is called saturated steam because it contains particles of water. Efficiency is improved if the water particles themselves are turned into steam by further heating out of contact with the boiler water. This is the function of the superheater. The steam pipe from the dome is led inside the boiler into the smokebox, where it feeds into the superheater header. From the upper section of the header a number of superheater elements extend back into the boiler inside large-diameter tubes which communicate with the firebox in the same way as the fire tubes already mentioned. Steam in the elements is therefore heated further by the hot gases flowing over them but is no longer in contact with the water. For maximum effect the elements are turned through 180 degrees so that having travelled as far as the firebox the steam is brought back again to the smokebox end, and then by further bends in the elements makes a second double journey to the firebox and back again. Finally it enters the lower portion of the superheater header, which is separated from the upper, or saturated steam, portion,

9

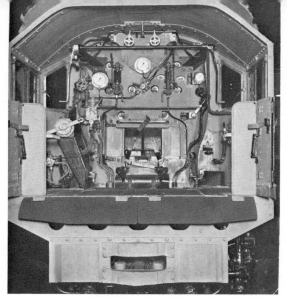

and is connected by steam pipes to the cylinders Assuming that steam in the boiler was at a pressure of 180lb/sq in and a temperature of 380 degrees F, it will emerge from the superheater at about 632 degrees F. The most important saving effected by superheating is in avoiding losses due to condensation when steam meets the cooler metal of the cylinder walls and the moisture particles in saturated steam are deposited as water.

For a more general appreciation of the advantages of superheating it must be remembered that heat is a form of energy. The locomotive converts the heat energy in the steam into mechanical energy, and the superheater increases the energy content of the steam.

The water in the boiler must always cover the crown of the inner firebox. As a precaution, plugs are fitted in the crown of the box which would melt in the intense heat if they were not covered, so that water would pour into the box and help to put the fire out. A water gauge in the cab shows the boiler water level and the driver sees that the supply is replenished as necessary from the reserve carried in tanks on the locomotive or in a separate tender. A locomotive that carries its water and coal on its own frames is called a tank locomotive. Usually the tanks are alongside the boiler, but sometimes they straddle it (saddle tank) or are below it (well tank). The initials ST and WT are used to denote the two last-named varieties. Coal for a tank locomotive is carried in a bunker behind the cab.

Water is fed into the boiler by injectors. Inside an injector steam from the boiler and the incoming water meet. The steam condenses so that a jet of mixed hot and cold water is formed. On passing through a cone of decreasing diameter, the jet is given a high velocity and is therefore able to force open a clack valve and enter the boiler against the pressure of the steam inside.

All the parts of the locomotive concerned with generating steam are lagged with asbestos-type material to minimise loss of heat. What one sees of the boiler and firebox when a locomotive is in service is in fact an outer casing painted and lined in the livery of the owning railway.

Just as a spring when compressed, or 'wound up', tries to expand and can be made to drive a mechanism, so does steam under pressure. When expansion takes place inside a cylinder containing a movable piston, the piston will be driven to the end of the cylinder remote from that at which the steam is admitted and so the energy in the steam is converted into mechanical energy.

For continuous motion steam has to be exhausted after each piston stroke and admitted at the opposite side of the piston to drive it back again. A rod attached to the piston passes through a steamtight gland in the front cover of the cylinder. The mechanism by which the to-and-fro motion of the piston rod is changed to rotary motion of the driving wheels is one of the most characteristic features of the steam locomotive and contributes much to the pleasure which so many people feel in seeing a locomotive at work.

The piston rod drives a crosshead which slides between slide bars. One end of a connecting rod is pivoted to the crosshead, and the other end is carried by a crankpin on a crank on the driving axle. If two or more axles have to be driven, their cranks are linked by coupling rods. A locomotive may have two, three or four cylinders. If there are only two they are inside the frames and the connecting rods are not easily visible, although the coupling rods between the leading and the other driving axles can be seen, the cranks being outside the wheels.

A further mechanism is necessary to drive the valves which control the admission and exhaust of steam. It takes various forms, but basically it imparts a rocking motion to a slotted link. One end of the valve operating rod is attached to a block which is a sliding fit in the link. The link moves the valve rod backwards and forwards as it rocks, and by changing the position of the block in the link the length of travel of the valve can be varied. By this means, also, the valve can be moved while the locomotive is stationary so that when steam is admitted it drives the locomotive forwards or backwards as required.

Before studying valve gears in more detail, the operation of the valve itself must be examined. The valve shown in Fig 2 is a piston valve, so called because it consists of two piston-type heads mounted some distance apart on the valve spindle. They slide to and fro inside a steamchest to which steam is admitted at both ends. The pistons being steam-tight, the steam cannot pass them so that the steamchest contains two 'pockets' of live steam which are admitted to the cylinder alternately as the ports are uncovered. Exhaust steam is discharged between the piston-heads, which separate it from the incoming live steam, and escapes through the blastpipe.

In Fig 2a the piston in the cylinder is moving to the left, steam being admitted through the right-hand port. Steam from the previous stroke is being exhausted through the left-hand port.

In Fig 2b the piston has reached the end of the stroke and is about to return to the right. Note that the piston valve has already been moving to the right, first closing the port on the left through which steam has been exhausted, then opening the same port again, but this time connecting it with the live steam in the left-hand end of the steam chest. Meanwhile the second piston-head has cut off the right-hand port from incoming steam and opened it to exhaust.

Live steam is not necessarily admitted throughout the piston stroke. By varying the valve travel by means of the valve gear the steam supply can be cut off after a certain percentage of the stroke so that for the rest of the stroke the steam in the cylinder works entirely by its expansive property. If cut-off takes place early, it is sometimes called working with a short cut-off, which is a confusing convention because the period during which steam is cut off is long and it is the admission period which is short. A better method is to express the point of cut-off as occurring after a certain percentage of the piston stroke. Thus 25% cut-off means that admission of steam to the cylinder is stopped when the piston has completed one-quarter of

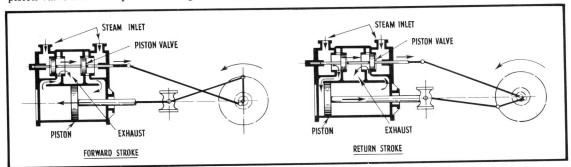

its travel. It has been calculated that the efficiency of working at about 12% cut-off is nearly twice that at 75%.

The valve gear shown in Fig 2 is purely schematic and would not allow for varying cut-off. A practical version is shown in Fig 3, being the familiar Walschaerts gear as applied to outside cylinders. The expansion link is the rocking link referred to earlier. It is given its rocking motion by the rod from the return crank fixed to the engine crankpin. The radius rod which drives the valve spindle is connected at the other end to a die block which can be moved up and down in the link by the reversing gear. It will be seen that the radius rod is not connected directly to the valve spindle but to a combination lever linked with the crosshead. These two systems act together in controlling the travel of the valve, the variable element being provided by the position of the die block in the expansion link. If, when the locomotive is stationary, the block is moved from one end of the link to the other, the valve itself will be shifted forwards or backwards so that when the regulator is opened steam is admitted at the side of the piston required for forward or reverse running. When the block is at the middle of the link, there is no effective movement of the valve and the engine is said to be in mid-gear.

The boiler and working parts of a locomotive are carried on main frames formed of steel plates about $1\frac{1}{16}$in thick. The side members of the frame structure are slotted to take the axleboxes of the driving axles, which can move up and down in the slots with the action of the springs. In the larger locomotives there are two axles under the smokebox to carry part of the

weight and help in guiding the locomotive on curves. They are mounted in a separate frame called a bogie which is connected with the main frames by a pivot so that it can align itself with curvature. The bogie centre casting which forms the lower part of the pivot is not fixed rigidly between the bogie frames but is allowed some degree of sideways travel so that the bogie can both rotate about its pivot and allow the locomotive to move laterally to one side or the other of the centre line of the track.

When there is a carrying axle under the firebox, as in Pacific or Atlantic locomotives, this also has some freedom to move sideways by special design of the axleboxes. Rear bogies were used in some large tank engines but were comparatively rare in British practice.

During the period of steam traction, most British railways used the vacuum brake. Vacuum has to be maintained to hold the brakes off while the train is running, and after a stop it must be recreated quickly to release the brakes. A small ejector on the locomotive works continuously for the first purpose (although sometimes mechanically driven pumps are used), and a large ejector provides for rapid establishment of vacuum. Both work on the same

Right: *Cleaned up for display at Swindon, open front end of GWR Dean 0-6-0 No 2516.*/M. Edwards

Below right: *Elegantly functional-looking motion of GWR 4-6-0 No 6000* King George V./R. C. H. Nash

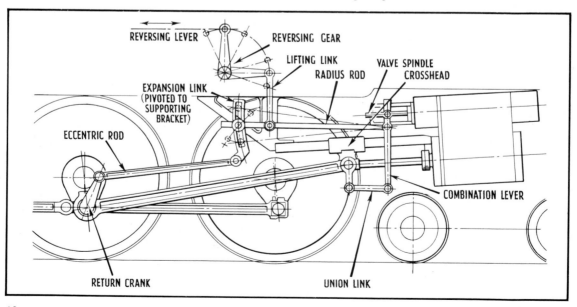

REVERSING LEVER
REVERSING GEAR
LIFTING LINK
RADIUS ROD
VALVE SPINDLE
CROSSHEAD
EXPANSION LINK (PIVOTED TO SUPPORTING BRACKET)
ECCENTRIC ROD
COMBINATION LEVER
RETURN CRANK
UNION LINK

principle. Steam from the boiler is discharged at high velocity through nozzles and expels air from a chamber connected with the train pipe. Pressure in the chamber therefore falls, causing air from the train pipe to flow into it and to be expelled with the steam.

When air is exhausted by the ejectors from the train pipe and the vacuum chambers and air cylinders connected to it throughout the train, the pressure in these parts of the system falls below that of the atmosphere. To apply the brakes, therefore, air at normal atmospheric pressure is admitted below the pistons in the brake cylinders and forces them upwards because of the lower pressure above them. As the pistons rise they apply brake blocks to the wheels through a system of cranks and rods.

The alternative to the vacuum brake is the air brake operated by air at above atmospheric pressure. The source of compressed air is a steam-driven pump, usually mounted on the side of the smokebox. In addition to air or vacuum brakes which work in conjunction with the brakes on the train, locomotives are provided with a handbrake acting on the engine and tender wheels, and often with a steam brake which either works automatically when the train brakes are applied or can be used independently.

Some of the controls used in driving a locomotive have been mentioned already. Regulator handles for admitting steam to the cylinders take various forms but are usually arranged so that the first movement opens a pilot valve which limits the supply, after which the main valve opens. The regulator is used in conjunction with the reverse gear controlling the valve travel. It is not to be thought of as a kind of accelerator in constant movement like that of a car, but as a control to be set in a position which, in combination with appropriate adjustment of the valve gear, enables the locomotive to maintain its schedule with maximum economy in the use of fuel. At one period locomotive valve gears were controlled by a large reversing lever working in a notched quadrant, but later practice was to use a screw adjustment with a cursor moving over a scale to show the condition of steam cut-off.

Water level in the boiler is shown in a glass tubular water gauge, and steam pressure by a dial-and-pointer type gauge graduated in pounds per square inch. A gauge of similar appearance shows the degree of vacuum in the brake system in 'inches of mercury'. This scale is based on the fact that normal atmospheric pressure will support a column of mercury 30in high. As air is withdrawn the height of the column that could be supported is reduced. In normal running with the brakes off the vacuum gauge shows about 20in of mercury, representing a pressure about 10lb below that of the atmosphere. The description 'vacuum' in the scientific sense is a misnomer, since a total vacuum cannot be created or maintained. Pressure gauges in air brake systems

normally read in the region of 70 to 80lb per sq in.

Keeping a locomotive in service involves many operations unseen by the traveller. On entering a depot at the end of a turn of duty the fire has to be dropped and ash and clinker disposed of. Ash accumulates in the smokebox as well as in the ashpan under the firegrate. At the same time the supply of sand used to check slipping on greasy rails will usually be replenished. At intervals the boiler has to be washed out and descaled, and the tubes cleaned. Specialised equipment for these purposes was developed as time went on, and in recent years tube cleaning has usually been performed while the locomotive is running, by blowing steam through them, sometimes combined with sand.

In the later years of steam traction major schemes of motive power depot modernisation were carried out, and much attention was given to water treatment, for the removal of impurities reduced the formation of scale, minimised corrosion and improved the efficiency of steam generation. Despite these improvements, the scope for extracting more work from the fuel consumed in the locomotive was limited, particularly within the limits imposed by the British loading gauge. In countries with more latitude in this respect, good results were obtained by compounding, that is, making the steam do work in a further cylinder or cylinders after being exhausted from those supplied at boiler pressure. These low-pressure cylinders had to be of greater volume and although the principle was used successfully in a few British designs it was probably seen at its best in Continental locomotives because of the larger dimensions within which the designer could work.

Technical progress could not change the fact that the by-products of burning coal create an environment that compares unfavourably with other and newer industries. In an age of pushbutton control, servo systems and sophisticated instrumentation the steam locomotive loses much of its glamour, and there are problems in recruiting staff to service and drive it. Perhaps if the energy crisis had been foreseen its life would have been extended, and more would have been done to apply the results of research which only became practicable with recent advances in technology. In some circumstances the fact of burning home-produced fuel could offset the low yield in mechanical energy from the heat energy released by combustion.

Facing page: Another study of motion, of LMS rebuilt Royal Scot Class 4-6-0 No 46132 The King's Regiment Liverpool. /Eric Treacy

Below: A sadder but perhaps more revealing view of a boiler's construction, as tubes are removed one by one from this scrapped LMS 2-8-0 in 1967./John H. Bird

Great Locomotives still at work

E. L. Cornwell

SOME READERS, no doubt, will, be at odds with the content of this and the following section of *Still in Steam*, finding their own favourite object of veneration inexplicably left out. To them I apologise, while asking them to remember the purpose of this book as stated in the introduction. Hence, here you will find not an exhaustive catalogue of all the preserved steam locomotives and carriages, nor a definitive description of preserved types, but a panoramic view across the field of working steam railway preservation, with glimpses of some of the wide variety of engines still in steam, and some of the early coaches still carrying passengers, and places where they may be seen and savoured.

Narrow-gauge articulated engine in Wales

Among the first of the lines, as opposed to individual locomotives, to be preserved were the several steam-hauled narrow-gauge Welsh railways, started with the formation in October 1950 of the Talyllyn Railway Preservation Society, which ran its first train on Whit Monday 1951. It was followed in 1951 by formation of the Festiniog Railway Society, which got the wheels turning again on a short section of the old slate-haulage line in 1955.

Most important of Festiniog's preserved locomotives, and among the handful of 19th-century engines still regularly working, are the two 0-4-4-0T Fairlies, *Merddyn Emrys* and *Iarll Meironwydd (Earl of Merioneth)*, built in the railway's own workshops in 1879 and 1885 respectively. These engines are called double Fairlies because each is in effect two complete steam engines mounted back to back on a single frame; the object was to obtain more pulling power than could be produced from a single conventional locomotive without incurring the heavy weight, wear and manning penalties of normal double heading.

The Fairlies are also of note for representing the earliest of the successful true articulated designs, first demonstrated on the steep Semmering line in Austria in 1851. An articulated locomotive is one in which one

Left: *Festiniog Railway 0-4-4-0T Fairlie* Merddyn Emrys *about to leave Porthmadog with a train for Dduallt in August 1973.* /R. E. B. Siviter

Above: *LBSCR 0-6-0 'Terrier', now KESR No 3* Bodiam, *with the Mayor of Tenterden and KESR Chairman up, during centenary celebrations in November 1972.*/Kent Messenger

or more driven axles, usually coupled groups of driven axles, can take up positions out of parallel with the others and can adjust to angular locations on curves, so providing an engine of high adhesive weight that can operate on curved track without excessive wear. Of the scores of articulated designs, most successful were the Mallets and Garratts, but single and double Fairlies and NBL Modified Fairlies made up a significant proportion of those put to use around the world.

Robert Fairlie's design for the Festiniog Railway was chiefly of interest because of its application to the narrow gauge of 1ft 11½in. Four of the 0-4-4-0T engines were built for the Festiniog. Each weighed 24tons and produced a tractive effort of just over 6000lb from 160psi boiler pressure supplying four 9½in by 14in cylinders driving 2ft 8in coupled wheels.

Veteran 0-6-0T in Kent

Even older than the Fairlies, and one of the oldest standard-gauge engines still at work in Britain, is the LBSCR 0-6-0T 'Terrier' *Bodiam* operated by the Kent & East Sussex Railway. It is one of the first two of the 50 Stroudley-designed Class A Terriers built by the old Brighton company between 1872 and 1880, and one of two of the class preserved in working order on the Kent & East Sussex Railway. The older of the two was built in October 1872, numbered 70 and named *Poplar*. It was sold by LBSCR to the KESR in 1901, to become No 3 *Bodiam* and to remain in service with the company until 1931.

Bodiam was earmarked for scrapping but instead it was rehabilitated, with parts from other cannibalised engines, and returned to service, surviving to undergo a rebuild to the later LBSCR A1X standard in 1943, and to pass into British Rail service on nationalisation. With the BR number 32670, the Terrier was moved to Eastleigh shed in 1954 to work the Hayling Island branch and continued there until the branch was closed in 1963. It was then purchased privately and is on permanent loan to the KESR. The 0-6-0T Terriers rebuilt to the A1X specification weighed 28¼tons and developed 7650lb tractive effort in two 12in by 20in cylinders, from a boiler pressure of 150psi and 4ft wheels.

17

Caley 0-4-4T at Falkirk

Although the first of the class was not completed until the year 1900, Caledonian Railway 0-4-4T No 419 operated by the Scottish Railway Preservation Society at Falkirk is typically 19th century in appearance and has the characteristic functional neatness of Caledonian engines. The 439 class of enlarged CR suburban and branch-line tank engines were designed by J. F. McIntosh and No 419 was delivered from St Rollox works, Glasgow, in 1907 as one of 68 of the class built between 1900 and 1914. Further batches, but with higher boiler pressures and bigger cylinders, were built under W. Pickersgill and the LMS up to 1925, to bring the grand total to 92.

The preserved engine saw such service working suburban traffic from Glasgow and was used for a time banking on Beattock. It passed into LMS service as No 15189 at the Grouping in 1923 and on to BR as No 55189 in 1947 with nationalisation, working successively from Ardrossan, Edinburgh and Glasgow before being withdrawn from service at Carstairs at the end of 1962. It was saved from the scrap heap through a public appeal by the Scottish RPS and finally restored to full working order in 1971.

The McIntosh 0-4-4T weighed 54tons and had 5ft 9in coupled wheels; it produced a tractive effort of 16,603lb from 18in by 26in cylinders and a maximum boiler pressure of 160psi.

GWR 2-6-2Ts in Devon

Almost the trademark of the Dart Valley Railway, though by no means its only ex-GWR working steam locomotive, is No 4555 — the 45xx class 2-6-2T (or Prairie tank) passenger engine introduced by G. J. Churchward in 1906. No 4555 was built in 1924 at Swindon and was one of a batch of 175 turned out between 1906 and 1929. In fact the 45xx class was one of a family of GWR 2-6-2 tank engines, including three successively bigger classes with 5ft 8in wheels for express passenger work and three classes with smaller wheels for branch-line work. The production run of the family extended from 1903 remarkably into the nationalisation era.

No 4555 had worked from many of the GWR sheds and was on the Ashburton branch in its later freight-only days up to the end of steam on BR; it had the distinction of working the last train out of Ashburton and of being the last engine in steam with BR Western

Region. It was acquired by DVR in October 1965.

The 45xx class engines had a weight of nearly 58 tons and developed 21,250lb tractive effort from two 17in by 24in cylinders and 200psi boiler pressure; coupled wheel diameter was 4ft 7½in.

In 1970, DVR acquired a second of the GWR Prairie tanks, No 4588 of the 4575 class, built in 1927, which has been restored to working condition and is regularly in traffic on the DVR. Its specification is generally as for the 45xx class except that water capacity is increased from 800 to 1300 gallons, carried in side tanks with sloping tops, which increases total weight to 61tons.

Below left: At Shildon on 31 August 1975 for the Railway 150th Anniversary Cavalcade, Caledonian Railway 0-4-4T No 419 takes its place with other steam veterans./John H. Bird

Right: A 15-coach Wirral Railway Circle special from Crewe in May 1972 was hauled from Totnes over the Dart Valley Line by GWR Prairie tanks Nos 4555 and 4588./G. R. Hounsell

Below: Another view of No 4588, this time working a regular train from Kingswear to Paignton in June 1977./G. A. Watt

Famous Flyer

Most famous of all preserved working steam locomotives is undoubtedly No 4472 *Flying Scotsman*, which is now housed at Steamtown, Carnforth. No 4472 was the third of the first batch of Gresley's Pacific express passenger locomotives for the LNER and was built at Doncaster in 1923 to Class A1 (later A10); No 4472 itself was later fitted with a higher-pressure boiler and other details developed for A3 class Pacifics.

This remarkable engine has numerous distinctions. It opened the London Kings Cross-Edinburgh 392.7mile non-stop Flying Scotsman train service in 1928, creating a new world record, and on the return run it achieved the first authenticated 100mph speed on British rails as well as averaging 80mph over a distance of 250 miles. For the long non-stop run special tenders were built with a corridor through from the locomotive cab to the first coach to permit changes of crew without stopping.

Flying Scotsman bore various numbers during its 40 years' service with the LNER and BR, ending its career in 1963 as No 60103. On withdrawal it was bought by Mr Alan Pegler and restored to LNER livery and the number 4472. Notable among its occasional runs on BR during that period was a repetition of the non-stop Kings Cross-Edinburgh run to mark the 40th anniversary of that event in May 1968. A major difference between the runs was that in 1968 a second tender had to be added to provide sufficient water for the run, water troughs from which tender tanks had been replenished on the move in steam days having gone out of use.

In 1969 the veteran engine was embarked by Mr Pegler on an ambitious tour of North America hauling a British trade exhibition train, but although it covered many miles the enterprise did not at the end have sufficient funds to bring *Flying Scotsman* home. Fears that it would end up in foreign possession, or worse as scrap, were eventually resolved when it was rescued by its present owner, Mr William McAlpine, and brought home to steam again on British rails.

As modified to Class A3, No 4472 has a boiler pressure of 220psi, three 19in by 26in cylinders and 6ft 8in driving wheels providing a tractive effort of 32,910lb, with weight of just over 96 tons.

Big and small GWR engines

Further examples of GWR locomotive art can be found working periodically at Didcot, where the GWR Society has two of the ubiquitous 57xx class 0-6-0PT engines, and at Hereford where the Bulmers Cider works maintains the big 4-6-0 King-class passenger express locomotive *King George V* owned by Swindon Corporation.

No 6000 *King George V* was the first of the class of big passenger engines introduced by GWR's C. B. Collett in 1927; like Churchward's Castle class before it, the King was the most powerful British locomotive of its day. A total of 30 was built between 1927 and 1929. *King George V* had the distinction of making a visit to the United States in 1927 for exhibition at the Fair of the Iron Horse organised by the Baltimore & Ohio Railroad; the mandatory bell fitted in the US continued to be carried after it returned home. Another point of interest is that the engine was built at Swindon in the remarkably short time of six months in order to meet the US commitment, then test-run on the

Below left: Most famous and most travelled of all preserved engines No 4472 Flying Scotsman, *towing little ancestor NER Fletcher 2-4-0 No 910, during the Shildon Cavalcade./M. Hall*

Right and below: Two views of GWR Collett 4-6-0 No 6000 King George V, *at Pontrilas on route for Newport in November 1972 (right) and near Church Stretton with a Salisbury-Newton Abbot special in September 1972./M. Pope, Tim Stephens*

Cornish Riviera Express, partially dismantled and packed and shipped inside a further two months. The engine was withdrawn from BR service in 1962 for preservation by Swindon Corporation at Swindon Museum; it is on loan to the Bulmer collection, which has restored it to full working condition.

The King-class engines weighed 89tons and had a tractive effort of 40,3000lb from a boiler pressure of 250psi, four 16¼in by 28in cylinders and 6ft 6in coupled wheels. Originally with single chimney, the Kings were fitted with double chimneys from 1955.

Also of Collett design are the little 0-6-0 pannier tank engines operated by the GWR Society at Didcot, representative of the prolific (and much-preserved) 57xx standard general-purpose class introduced on the GWR in 1929. The 57xx class, which itself was designed to replace several older similar classes, was the second largest class of locomotives ever produced in the UK, reaching a total production of over 860 between 1929 and 1946. A batch of the GWR engines was bought by London Transport for hauling works trains and some of them continued in service into the 1970s, several years after the end of working steam on British Rail.

The 57xx class engines weighed 47½tons and had a boiler pressure of 200psi, two 17½in by 24in cylinders and 4ft 7½in wheels, and produced 22,515lb tractive effort. The number of the class preserved runs into double figures. The two engines of the GWR Society,

Nos 3650 and 3738, were built at Swindon in the late 1930s.

Black Fives

Also representative of a very successful, very numerous and now much preserved class in No 5231, one of the Stanier Class 5 4-6-0s — the famous Black Fives, maintained by the Main Line Steam Trust at Loughborough. About a dozen Black Fives are preserved and about half of them are steamed from time to time, including at Carnforth Steamtown, Severn Valley Railway, Keighley & Worth Valley Railway and North Yorkshire Moors Railway.

The LMS Class 5 design is generally considered to be the most versatile and useful steam locomotive ever produced in the UK and after nationalisation there was scarcely a line in the country on which they did not serve. It was the third most numerous British class, with a total of 842 built at various works between 1934 and 1950, No 5231 having come from an Armstrong Whitworth batch of 1936-38. More Black Fives than any other class continued to run on BR to the end of steam in 1967, and Stanier's general design was also the basis of the BR standard Class 5 4-6-0, of which 172 were built between 1951 and 1957.

The Black Fives could apply 25,455lb tractive effort through 6ft wheels from two 18½in by 28in cylinders and 225psi boiler pressure; working weight of the engine was just over 72tons.

Left: *Another Collett design and one of the Great Western Society's two 0-6-0PTs, No 3738 at Didcot in April 1977.* /N. E. Preedy

Right and below: *Two pictures of one of the numerous preserved LMS Stanier Black Fives, 4-6-0 No 5231 working trains for the Main Line Steam Trust at Loughborough in October 1973.*/both W. K. Squires

24

From the Streamline era

LMS 4-6-2 Pacific No 6233 *Duchess of Sutherland* maintained at Bressingham Hall in Norfolk is one of three preserved Stanier Coronation-class passenger express engines, some of which originally appeared with streamlined casings. Two of these handsome and powerful engines, 38 of which were built between 1937 and 1948, were bought after withdrawal from BR service by the Butlin's concern, No 6229 *Duchess of Hamilton* to be displayed at the company's Minehead holiday camp and No 6233 at the Ayr establishment. No 6229 is now to be on view at the York Railway Museum and No 6233 a few years ago went to the Bressingham Live Steam Museum, where it underwent extensive repair and now remains on permanent loan.

The Coronation Pacifics were among the three or four most powerful steam locomotives ever to run in Britain, producing 40,000lb tractive effort from four 16¼in by 28in cylinders and 250psi boiler pressure. Weight was just over 105tons in final form but those that originally appeared with streamlined casings weighed about three tons more.

Pacific in Miniature

No less imposing in its own scale, though standing only shoulder height to the average man, is the 15in-gauge Pacific *Black Prince* recently placed in regular passenger service by the Romney, Hythe & Dymchurch Railway in Kent. The engine is one of three similar built in Essen, Germany, in 1937 by the Krupp company to a basic design by Henry Greenly for an exhibition park in Düsseldorf. After similar use at Munich and Cologne they were put into store in 1967, from which two were brought in 1972 for a new Bressingham 15in-gauge line, retaining their German names *Rosenkavalier* and *Männertreu*, and the third in 1977 by RHDR, to take its new (traditional) RHDR name, and to start work in April 1977.

Facing page: *LMS Stanier Coronation Pacific No 6233* Duchess of Sutherland *spick and span and in steam again in the care of Bressingham Steam Museum in July 1975.*/J. H. Cooper-Smith

Below: *Two views of the German-built miniature Pacific* Black Prince *during its first day in service with Romney, Hythe & Dymchurch Railway in September 1976.*/R. E. Ruffell

War Department's biggest

The War Department's main big goods engine in WW2 was the so-called Austerity version of the Stanier 8F 2-8-0 developed by R. A. Riddles. Many hundreds were built in the works of all four of the main railways and by several private manufacturers for service in many countries. To meet the need for similar heavy hauling capacity on lighter or war-damaged track Mr Riddles also developed a 2-10-0 version of the locomotive which had similar tractive effort of over 34,000lb yet was capable of negotiating tight curves and had an axle loading of 13½tons. The engine had no flanges on the middle driving wheels and only shallow flanges on the second and fourth coupled wheel pairs.

The WD 2-10-0 was introduced in 1943 and up to 1945 150 were built, all by North British Locomotive

Left and below: WD Riddles 2-10-0 heavy hauler No 600 Gordon, *awaiting attention at Bewdley, SVR, in November 1971 and heading a regular SVR train in May 1974.* /Anthony A. Vickers, D. A. Idle

Below right: Bulleid West Country Pacific No 34023 Blackmore Vale *with a Sheffield Park-Horsted Keynes train on its inaugural run on the Bluebell line in May 1976.*/Brian Morrison

Company. The second engine in the production run, turned out in December 1943 and numbered 3651, was delivered to the WD railway training centre at Longmoor. It remained there throughout its working life on training work, one of the few WD 2-10-0s that did not serve abroad; it was renumbered 73651 in 1944 and given its present number of 600 and the name *Gordon* in 1952. When Longmoor Military Railway closed down *Gordon* was acquired by the Transport Trust and is now operated by Severn Valley Railway, Bridgnorth.

The WD 2-10-0 produced 34,215lb tractive effort from 19in by 28in cylinders and 225psi pressure; it weighed 78½tons and had 4ft 8½in coupled wheels.

Bulleid Light Pacific

Probably no controversy in railway circles has ever been greater or more prolonged than that generated by the various designs of O. V. S. Bulleid. Fortunately numbers of Bulleid-designed locomotives have been preserved and can still be seen working, including the Southern Railway West Country Pacific No 34023 *Blackmore Vale* maintained in original unrebuilt form on the Bluebell Railway.

The Bulleid Pacifics were unconventional in respects other than design, not least the numbering, which prefaced the usual running number with the class designation 2IC1. They were also notable for being given the go-ahead during wartime in the face of a general ban on building anything but freight engines, which they obviously were not. By describing them as mixed-traffic type the Southern got round the embargo and 20 of the earlier Merchant Navy class were built between 1941 and 1945, with 10 more following in 1948-49. When further new locomotives were required in 1945 for secondary non-electrified routes a lighter version of the design with a smaller boiler was introduced and named West Country class, of which no fewer than 110 were built.

The Bulleid Pacifics were sparkling performers but at the expense of high coal consumption and maintenance costs largely brought about by an unconventional valve gear. Eventually, from 1956 on, the whole of the Merchant Navy class and 60 of the West Country class were rebuilt to eliminate the troubles, losing the original air-smoothed casings as seen on *Blackmore Vale*.

The West Country Pacific class, which included the series of engines given Battle of Britain names, starting with *Winston Churchill*, which is preserved by BR, could produce 27,715lb tractive effort from three $16\frac{3}{8}$in by 24in cylinders and a pressure of 250psi. Driving wheels were 6ft 2in in diameter and the engine weight was 86tons.

Left: *Peppercorn K1 2-6-0 No 2005 working a train from Goathland at Grosmont (above) and at Goathland on its inaugural run on NYMR in June 1974./both Brian Morrison*

Above: *BR 2-6-4T No 80002 at Haworth, KWVR, in June 1969 after removal from Glasgow./Ian G. Holt*

LNER Peppercorn Mogul

The Peppercorn Class K1 2-6-0 No 2005 owned by the North Eastern Locomotive Preservation Group and operated by the North Yorkshire Moors Railway is interesting for being preserved in a livery which it never bore in service. The Peppercorn Mogul did not appear until after nationalisation, 70 numbered 62001-62070 having been built in 1949 and 1950, but it was essentially a LNER design with a lineage reaching back to the original Great Northern 2-6-0 produced at Doncaster Works in 1912.

That original GN K1 was followed by several variations on the 2-6-0 mixed-traffic theme up to the LNER's K4 designed by Sir Nigel Gresley to cope with the severe operating conditions of the West Highland line. Peppercorn's K1 was a direct development of a Thompson 1945 rebuild of a Gresley K4. To provide the high tractive effort required for the West Highland gradients the K4 had three 18½in by 26in cylinders, compared with two 20in by 26in cylinders of the K2 class, which had worked the line

previously, and a wheel diameter reduced from the earlier 5ft 8in to 5ft 2in. The LNER K1 reverted to the two 20in cylinders but retained the smaller wheels, providing a tractive effort of 32,080lb with a boiler pressure of 225psi.

A Gresley K4, No 3442 *The Great Marquess*, is owned by Lord Garnock and kept on the Severn Valley Railway.

BR Standard Passenger Tank

Also directly descended from a long line of company developments of a single wheel-formation theme is BR standard 2-6-4T No 80002 maintained in working order on the Keighley & Worth Valley Railway. The BR standard passenger tank engine, of which 155 were built at the Brighton, Derby and Doncaster works between 1951 and 1957, is a direct descendant of a line of locomotives of similar configuration and purpose dating back to Fowler and Stanier in the early years of the LMS.

Being of relatively recent vintage, the BR 2-6-4Ts have been fairly accessible and about 10 have been saved from scrapping and preserved. Keighley's example, No 80002, which was built at Derby and worked mainly on Glasgow suburban train services, was retained for a while after withdrawal of steam in Scotland in 1966, and used as a carriage heating boiler at Cowlairs. It was bought by the KWVR Preservation Society in 1969.

The class had 18in by 28in cylinders, a boiler pressure of 225psi and 5ft 8in wheels, with a weight of 88½tons, and developed a tractive effort of 25,100lb.

Focus on Preserved Coaches

G. M. Kichenside

APART FROM the pioneer narrow-gauge preserved lines, where coaches were sometimes left standing when original services ceased, so that rolling stock of a sort could be made available for reopening, groups taking on standard-gauge lines, right from the start were faced with the purchase of coaches from British Railways to operate passenger services. Indeed it almost seemed as though coaches were an afterthought in the early years of railway preservation.

In the last decade, though, attitudes have changed, and many railway carriages have been preserved for their value in representing particular periods of design or to make up complete trains of a single company's types. Even the official national collection of preserved rolling stock sadly has gaps in its coverage and a casual visitor might be forgiven for thinking that most of our great grandparents travelled in either spartan four-wheelers of the 1830s or opulent private saloons.

It is a pity that carriage preservation did not get off the ground much earlier, for many representatives of the turn of the century survived the second world war, but not for long. A few examples of that era which managed to survive have been rescued not from active public service but usually as engineering department mess vehicles, often much altered and certainly not in the best of condition. Interiors were frequently gutted

so that restoration has almost meant building a new interior inside the outer shell. Exceptions have been the saloons which have survived in BR service for use by departmental managers and engineers on line inspections, but they are not typical of the coaches used by the travelling public.

Thus one looks in vain for more than one or two preserved examples of notable types from mid- and late-Victorian years, and from much of the Edwardian period. How splendid it would be to compare a real Midland clerestory 12-wheeler of 1874, the first standard-gauge British bogie vehicle, with the first side-corridor six-wheeler from the East Coast Joint stock; or to see the luxury of a Midland Pullman of the same period side-by-side with one of the South Eastern & Chatham Folkestone vestibule cars, or the Edwardian opulence of the LNWR's American boat train first-class coaches with their drawing rooms. But of even greater interest, what were the Great Western's broad-gauge coaches really like? Alas! We of the twentieth century will never know (unless someone at Didcot gets out the drawings and builds one together with *Iron Duke* as a project for the centenary in 1992 of the end of the broad gauge!).

This feature illustrates some of the many coaches that have survived and which in many cases have been lovingly restored to illustrate some of the best (and the worst) coaches that have run in Britain.

The National Railway Museum at York, opened on a new site in 1975, houses an interesting collection of coaches but because of limited space not all the preserved vehicles can be displayed and some are still in store. On the turntable are two replica coaches built in 1930 for the centenary of the Liverpool & Manchester Railway. In the foreground to the left is the Bodmin & Wadebridge first-/second-class composite of 1834, the horse-drawn Port Carlisle dandy, a composite coach of the Stockton & Darlington Railway and a handsome collection of saloons, travelling post office coaches and a 1910 Pullman car. One of the recent additions to the collection is a Midland six-wheel composite of 1885 which besides showing the advance in comfort for third-class passengers, pioneered by the Midland, also has a remarkable resemblance in many aspects of its appearance to LMS bogie non-corridor coaches which survived until the end of the steam era. Fortunately this Midland composite coach fills a gap in late-Victorian designs and, surprisingly, survived undamaged and unaltered until recent years. It was sold by the Midland Railway just after the first world war to an industrial concern at Manchester for use on workmen's trains on its private system and was rescued for preservation in the 1950s.

The Midland was to the forefront of passenger comfort, having abolished second class in the 1870s and upgraded the furnishing of third-class compartments to include padded seats, almost unheard of at that time on most lines. Midland six-wheelers such as that illustrated were used on main-line long-distance services until the end of the decade and a broadly similar body profile and general design were used for bogie stock until the Midland introduced the massive Clayton clerestory coaches in the late 1890s./Crown Copyright, National Railway Museum

31

The Bluebell Railway, the first of the standard-gauge preserved passenger lines, has acquired a fascinating collection of coaches from a variety of companies, although in the last few years the railway has been strengthening its Southern image. This 1970s shot shows (top left) stock built by four different companies; leading next to the engine is the former London & South Western observation car, originally built just before the first world war for scenic trips on the Blaenau Ffestiniog branch and now used by the Bluebell to show the glories of the Sussex countryside. Second is a South Eastern & Chatham third-class coach, technically a Southern rebuild on a new underframe in the 1920s using old bodies; third is a Southern open third of the Maunsell era, a pattern sometimes used as dining cars, and at the end of their BR days as push-pull coaches for branch work; fourth is a highly unlikely type in the south of England, a Caledonian Railway corridor third, since repatriated to Scotland in exchange for an exiled Southern coach, and bringing up the rear a South Eastern & Chatham birdcage brake third. The Bluebell's observation car is not the only observation vehicle to be preserved for one of the two Devon Belle cars is on the Dart Valley — see page 43 — (the other car is in America) and both the LNER Coronation cars have been preserved.

Above is a closer view of the Caledonian third in its native territory and left is the South Eastern & Chatham brake third. Prominent is the birdcage guard's lookout above the main roof. The birdcage is of considerable antiquity in railway use for it stems right from the start of railways when the guards and brakemen sat high up at the coach ends to see over the roofs for signals either from the lineside or the engine to apply the brakes. Soon, for safety reasons the guard's positions were enclosed by glassed-in observatories above the main roof. Because of limited clearances for side lookouts the South Eastern & Chatham retained the raised observatory almost to the end of its existence and many of these coaches survived until the early 1960s.
/ J. H. Cooper Smith, John H. Bird, G. P. Stilley, Brian Morrison, J. H. Cooper Smith.

East Coast Joint Stock corridor third-class coach No 12 is one of the few preserved representatives of the late Victorian period when so much in railway carriage design and train comfort was undergoing change. Until the 1890s main-line trains were still formed largely of six-wheel coaches without corridors, mostly even without toilet facilities, and certainly without on-train refreshments except on the few Pullman services. A decade later had seen the introduction on a wide scale of bogie coaches, corridors, and dining cars, as part of the competition between companies to improve the quality of travel.

One of the design features prominent at this time was the clerestory roof, the raised centre portion with windows along the sides. The clerestory was not a long-lived form of construction in railway carriages but it became so typical of turn-of-the-century vehicles that it is difficult to realise that its peak years generally lasted no more than a decade from the mid 1890s to about 1905, although the Midland and Great Western employed it at

intervals for much longer and many companies did not use it at all.

The Great Northern Railway, and coaches built for the East Coast Joint Stock, a pool of vehicles provided specially for through workings between London and Scotland over the lines of the three East Coast companies, had a particularly graceful form of clerestory roof curving down to meet the coach ends.

ECJS No 12 was in fact built by the North Eastern Railway but to broadly GNR pattern. Like other East Coast stock it was fitted with automatic couplers more than 50 years before BR standardised the type for its new corridor stock in the 1950s. No 12 is one of the relics forming part of the official national collection but because of a shortage of space at York Railway Museum it is stored at the time of writing despite its greater historical significance than some of the exhibits on show in the museum./British Rail

Between them the Severn Valley Railway, Great Western Society and Dart Valley Railway have a fine collection of Great Western coaches covering many periods, from Dean clerestory coaches of the turn of the century to the last GW Hawksworth types built after the second world war. Indeed the groups responsible for restoration have carried out some really top-class work in bringing to life GWR chocolate and cream in all its glory. On this Severn Valley train of 1970 are two corridor coaches of the late 1930s next to the engine, third is one of the ocean saloons built for the Plymouth-London boat trains in 1931, fourth is a post-war corridor third, followed by an early WW2 composite and brought up at the rear by an early 1930s brake third of the type retaining side doors to each compartment.

Close-up shows the fine restoration carried out on GWR corridor composite No 7285 on the Severn Valley Railway. This was one of the few coaches built during the second world war in a batch of 20 completed in 1941. They were 59ft 10in long, 8ft 11in wide and included four first-class and three third-class compartments.

With little doubt among the best known Great Western coaches are the 'super saloons' built in 1931/2 for ocean liner boat trains between Plymouth and Paddington. They are certainly well to the fore in preservation circles for of the eight built originally no fewer than five are in private hands, two on the Dart Valley and, following a transfer from the SVR, three at the Great Western Society's depot at Didcot. The were also among the largest coaches ever built for a British main-line railway, with a body width of 9ft 7in, seven inches wider than the normal maximum for universal use on British Railways, and resulting from the generous loading-gauge clearances bequeathed to the Great Western in the twentieth century by the broad gauge. They had a similar body profile to the 1935 'centenary' stock for the Cornish Riviera and only the 1904 GW Dreadnought stock was bigger, for although the width was an inch narrower, lengths were 68-70ft compared with the 61ft 4½in of the super saloons.

Internally the super saloons rivalled Pullman cars in their appointments, with walnut veneers, Wilton carpet and individual wing armchairs, in pairs or in fours, with tables between. A typical Pullman touch was the table lamp, and the small four-seat coupé compartments independent of the main saloons. Two of the super saloons were later rebuilt with kitchens which overcame the need for a separate kitchen or restaurant car.

Externally the super saloons look massive and are distinguished with their angled recessed wide end doors, which unusually are hinged towards the centre of the coach instead of the normal left-hand hinge. Today the latest BR coaches with their wide wraprounc end doors have the reverse arrangement with the hinge at the outer end. *Illustrated below is* Prince of Wales, *No 9113* ./John Hunt, John H. Bird, C. R. Jenkins

Without doubt more Great Western coaches have been preserved than from any other railway and few periods of GWR carriage design in the present century are unrepresented. Moreover there are examples from practically all types of service including ordinary main-line corridor stock, diners, sleepers, saloons, non-corridor local stock, and branch line vehicles. In the latter category come the Great Western's ubiquitous auto-trailers, once the mainstay of many GWR branch and a few main-line stopping services. Singly, in pairs, or more rarely in fours as on Plymouth suburban services, they trundled back and forth in company with a small tank engine, usually one of the 14XX 0-4-2Ts or a pannier, making connections at junctions with long-distance express services. The Great Western auto-train was as much a part of the western railway scene as Kings and Castles.

The auto-cars had their origins in the steam railmotors introduced soon after the turn of the century in an attempt to reduce operating costs to compete with electric trams in the bigger towns and, even then, the looming motor vehicle. The railmotor was simply a self-propelled carriage containing a small steam engine unit at one end. Those of the Great Western looked just like a carriage but other railways did not disguise the power unit and it was dressed up as a minute four-wheeled steam locomotive outside the coach body. The small power unit was designed to run economically with minimum coal and water consumption and thus had little in reserve for attachment of extra coaches. Often not more than one additional coach could be hauled, a drawback at times of heavy traffic.

The steam railmotor survived the first world war but by then most railways had turned to the push-pull train which, with a more conventional tank engine, which could be detached for other work when required, was a more flexible arrangement. Some of the GWR steam railmotors were rebuilt as trailer coaches for push-pull working and others were built new. They were rather austere inside but journeys were usually short. They had open saloon interiors, a driving cab at one end from which the driver could operate remotely the locomotive regulator and the train brake, a guard's and luggage compartment at the other,

while the one passenger door on each side had folding steps underneath which could be opened out by the guard at halts not provided with raised platforms.

Several GWR auto-cars have been preserved, mostly the post-war type which were not in fact built until the 1950s several years after the GWR had ceased to exist. Again, examples can be seen at three main preserved centres following GWR practice, the Severn Valley, Didcot GW Society depot and the Dart Valley lines in South Devon. Although the Dart Valley coaches are in regular service they are not used for push-pull duties largely because push-pull trains are limited to only two or three vehicles which in today's conditions would be an uneconomic working, and because few DVR engines originally fitted for auto working still have the equipment available./Eric Knight, Peter Zabek

The South Eastern & Chatham Railway routes to the Kent coast were short compared with the northern main lines from London and even the East Kent resorts and ports were within 80 miles of the capital. So the SECR did not join the rush into corridor stock at the end of the 1890s and was content to continue with non-corridor stock, even on its principal expresses and what, in effect, were international services between London and the Channel ports of Folkestone and Dover on the first (or last) leg of journeys to France and beyond. The SECR did bow to public need by providing some of its coaches with between-compartment toilets, some with access only from one compartment, others with short side corridors linking two or three compartments but not with inter-coach gangways. Usually the first- and second-class compartments were fairly well endowed with such facilities but the thirds less so. Indeed, lower-class passengers, often with children, would have needed to be very experienced in South Eastern carriage designs to identify the compartments with toilet access for they were not marked externally.

Apart from some gangwayed brake tri-composites built in the early years of the century for through workings from the Kent Coast to the Midlands and North, and its forays with its saloon 'car' trains in the 1890s, the SECR remained without corridor stock almost to the end of its existence in 1922; almost, because right at the end there came a batch of gangwayed coaches quite unlike anything that had appeared on the SECR before. They were longer at 62ft than previous types, though the SECR had got as far as 60ft by about 1913, with straight-sided bodies, matchboarded below the waist. They had end doors rather than individual doors to compartments, a feature tried by the GWR nearly 20 years earlier but which had not then caught

on. For a number of reasons, partly because of their intended use, and partly because of looks, these new SEC corridor vehicles were known as 'continental stock'. There were several types of coach and the brake firsts even included a feature so beloved by the SECR, a small first-class saloon. The brake thirds were more conventional and one has been preserved, of all places on the Keighley & Worth Valley Railway. The photograph shows it next to former USA class 0-6-0T No 72 on the KWVR, and the other shows a similar coach in Southern excursion use in the 1950s./ J. B. Mounsey ,G. M. Kichenside

Even though the first bogie coaches in Britain had appeared in the 1870s their general introduction for long-distance services was gradual and it was not until the development of through corridors and dining cars that they became more widespread during the 1890s. For suburban services it was a different matter and four-wheelers were still common well after the turn of the century around most cities. Among the first users of bogie coaches from 1898 for suburban trains was the Metropolitan for its workings between London, Chesham and Verney Junction (the latter completed in 1897) at first worked by a mixture of four-wheelers and rigid eight-wheelers. The 1898 stock, mainly built by the Ashbury C & W Co with three classes of accommodation, was quite short at 39ft 6in but was otherwise neat and workmanlike, with a low arc roof typical of the last century. Their length incidentally gives a distinctive sound when running, for, unlike a 57-60ft coach which gives the familiar four-beat di-di-di-dum rhythm on 60ft jointed track, and a 48-50ft coach with a five-beat pattern because an extra axle is involved in the railjoint sequence, these Metropolitan Ashbury coaches coupled as a set manage to get six axles on a 60ft rail with, in consequence, a six-beat rhythm.

Unusually, too, the preserved examples (and five of the six surviving in London Transport stock in 1960 have been retained), started life hauled by steam locomotives, were converted to electric multiple-units, and were later converted back to steam push-pull operation. All of the original batches were converted at intervals to electric operation for the Metropolitan electrification programme and the opening of new branches to Uxbridge in 1904, Watford in 1925 and Stanmore in 1932. Six coaches were converted for steam push-pull use for the Chesham branch during the second world war, and while the remainder of the type in use as electric stock were scrapped soon after the war and replaced by modern stock, the six push-pull coaches survived on the Chesham branch for 20 years until it, too, was electrified in 1961. It was just at that time that the Bluebell Railway was looking for coaches and four of the Chesham coaches saw service between Sheffield Park and Horsted Keynes. Their age however is beginning to show for they are nearly 80 years old and they are stored at present pending further work on them in the light of the Bluebell's future rolling stock needs. The fifth coach, at the time of writing, is being restored for display at London Transport's Syon Park Museum.

Some examples of later Metropolitan coaches have also been preserved, from the various batches of 51-foot stock built between 1910 and 1923. Again they were very much like suburban stock of the main-line companies with high elliptical roofs but they continued a Met tradition with round-topped doors, and the third-class compartments were much more cramped at 5ft 6in between compartment partitions, compared with the 6ft or more of many other lines. Three coaches — a third, brake third, and a first — are on the Keighley & Worth Valley Railway.
/P. J. Sharpe, J. B. Mounsey

Oliver Bulleid, chief mechanical engineer of the Southern Railway, was noted for his many innovations in steam locomotive design. In coaching stock, too, he developed many new ideas, particularly in the design of suburban electric stock, where he aimed to cram as many passengers as possible in minimum space. Perhaps he overdid it in his first coaches of the 1940s, but his development of steel body framing certainly helped to add an inch or so to interior widths even though the interiors were rather austere and there was little space for sound and thermal insulation. Bulleid's post-war main-line stock for the SR followed much the same pattern as the suburban stock but was less spartan. The same all-steel body sides were employed, notable for their continuous curve from top to bottom, instead of straight above the waist with a tumblehome curve beneath, traditional on British stock. Windows had well-rounded corners, and doors had a top light above the drop window which was self balancing and did away with the need for window straps.

Surprisingly Bulleid stuck to timber and canvas roofs for his main-line stock, despite all-steel bodies on his suburban electric units. He introduced a new length to the Southern with 63ft 5in underframes and new interior layouts with end and centre doors, and some coaches with both open saloon and compartment accommodation. Many design features were taken up in the early 1950s when the BR standard all-steel coaches were on the drawing board. Several Bulleid main-line coaches have been preserved, nearly all on the Bluebell Railway, which is gradually developing a predominantly Southern image. Two are seen next to USA tank No 30064 at Sheffield Park./Brian Morrison

Soon after the turn of the century several railways started looking at ways of reducing operating costs on lightly used branch services. Several investigated steam railcars, usually single coaches powered by a small steam engine unit designed to run very economically with low fuel consumption. Because of their low power they were not able to cope with heavy traffic on

peak days since few could haul additional coaches. A few railways experimented with internal-combustion railcars but they were unreliable at that time. It was not until the 1930s that the diesel engine made a general appearance for rail traction use, for until that time the restraining factor had been the lack of a suitable transmission. The Great Western, pioneer of steam railcars in the first decade, was also the pioneer of diesel railcars in the 1930s using a mechanical transmission with a multi-speed gearbox. The GW diesel railcars were an outstanding success, not only on branch services, but also on stopping services on main lines. One or two were fitted with toilet and buffet facilities and were used on fast inter-city express duties, particularly between Birmingham and Cardiff. Yet on this route their popularity was their undoing, for traffic outstripped their capacity and they had to be replaced by locomotive-hauled trains.

When British Rail was drawing up plans for the start of the general dieselisation programme in the mid 1950s, the experience gained over 20 years with the GW railcars was very much in mind when the BR diesel multiple-unit fleet was being evolved. Most of the BR units were formed as two- or three-car sets rather than the single cars of most of the GWR types. No fewer than three of the GW cars have been preserved, one each located at Didcot and the Severn Valley Railway, but remarkably also one on the Kent & East Sussex Railway.

Apart from the diesel multiple-units BR also tried out four-wheel diesel railbuses on a few branch lines in an endeavour to cut costs, but they were doomed to failure because if traffic was light enough to be carried by a railbus there could not be sufficient revenue to cover a line's overall costs. Nevertheless although most were out of service by the mid 1960s after a life of less than six years, no fewer than six have been preserved, four German-built cars by Waggon und Maschinenbau, two of which operate on the Keighley & Worth Valley Railway, and two by AC cars. One of the W&M cars is seen at Haworth, while GW car No 22 is seen at Bridgnorth./David M. Cross, Ian G. Holt

Edward Thompson, Gresley's successor as chief mechanical engineer of the LNER, was well known for his new policies in locomotive design after the second world war but perhaps less so for his new coaching stock types, which broke away from traditional Gresley practice. Corridor stock for long-distance services in particular, built from 1945, brought new thinking into internal layouts to improve passenger access. Right up to the second world war the LNER had continued to build corridor coaches with side doors to each compartment even though Gresley had opted for end doors with corridor access to compartments for some of his corridor vehicles for set trains and the streamlined sets of the mid 1930s. Thompson thought the difficulty of passengers entering a coach by end doors and struggling along a corridor with cases to a centre compartment could be overcome by repositioning the end doors and transverse vestibules towards the centre of the coach, breaking the compartments into groups of two-three-two in the corridor thirds, and into twos for the composite and first-class coaches.

Thus passengers needed to pass at most only one other compartment in getting to and from the external doors. These vehicles also introduced for general production steel-panelled bodies (some steel-panelled coaches had been produced in Gresley's time) but they continued the teak livery which was painted in grained form even though plain brown was used on some of the older pre-grouping coaches. Oval toilet windows gave them a distinctive appearance. Although the Thompson stock was built for a short period they became a well recognised part of the post-war LNER scene. Thompson's non-corridor stock, in contrast, was little different from pre-war practice except in length, 52ft 2in underframes against Gresley's 51ft, but had steel panels and were similar in appearance to Thompson's corridor stock. Few of Thompson's coaches have been preserved but seen here on the North Yorkshire Moors line is a 52ft non-gangwayed lavatory composite with internal corridors, and a 58ft corridor composite./G. M. Kichenside, John Hunt, D. L. Percival

Post-WW2 coaches on the LMS visually showed little difference from that company's products of the 1930s, yet there were important detail changes. Principal was the adoption of all-steel body construction with steel frames and bodyside panels welded to form a much stronger body than the timber-framed steel-panelled type standard on the LMS during the previous decade or so. The LMS, like the LNER, changed the design of toilet windows, and the corresponding windows on the corridor side, from the normal rectangular shape to a circular pattern and gave post-war coaches to which they were fitted the nickname 'porthole' stock. They were built for only about five years, for nationalisation brought new designs, yet they also became associated distinctively with this short period of LMS history. A corridor composite of this pattern has been preserved on the Severn Valley Railway in company with similar Stanier-designed coaches of pre-war days to form a typical LMS corridor set, seen here hauled by Ivatt Class 2 2-6-0 No 46443./British Rail, D. C. Williams

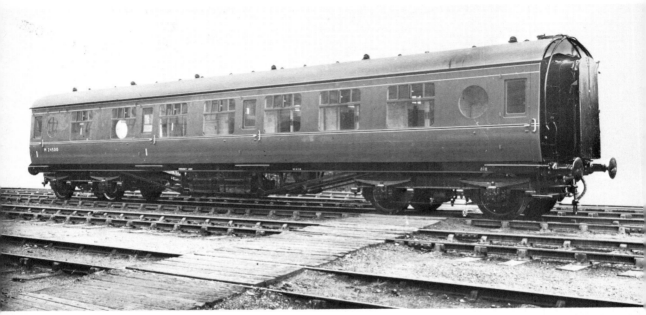

It may be asked why preservation societies would want to preserve coaches which are still currently very much in use on British Railways. Yet numerous examples of the BR standard-pattern coaches of the 1950s, both corridor and non-corridor, are running on several private railways. There are several reasons: first, for a railway looking simply for any type of coach for carrying passengers, and not one with historical value, the BR open second is as good a coach as any; secondly, they will probably be in better condition than earlier examples, although corrosion of body panels is something that might have to be reckoned with; thirdly, there is little else left which would be immediately usable for a line setting up in recent years; and finally, the Mk I pattern BR coaches are already 20-25 years old and will soon have a historical significance. BR non-corridor coaches already are historical relics, for locomotive-hauled non-corridor trains are now virtually a thing of the past on BR. The BR standard coach of the 1950s was not remarkable in its accommodation for it showed little improvement from the best of the design practices of the four group companies. Essentially it was a safer coach with a strong steel body welded to the underframe to form a solid box structure. Combined with buckeye centre couplers this type of coach has stood up well in accidents. BR standard coaches are seen on a train of the Lakeside & Haverthwaite Railway, and in company with the Devon Belle observation car at Buckfastleigh on the Dart Valley Railway./Peter J. Skelton, L. A. Nixon

Running a Preserved Railway

G. M. Kichenside
Commercial Manager, Dart Valley Railway

IN PRE-GROUPING DAYS general managers of the individual railways were often eminent personages running *their* railway with an iron fist, and in a few cases with an organisation run on as near dictatorship lines as it was possible to get. Others were firm but kindly rulers, presiding over practically all parts of the railway, except possibly the specialist engineering departments. Some of these officers were well known and a few progressed in later life to become company chairmen, and continued very much in day-to-day control of the entire railway, sometimes even more than one railway. Few will not have heard of Sir Edward Watkin who ruled over the Manchester, Sheffield & Lincolnshire and the South Eastern; there was also James Milne of the Great Western, the redoubtable Herbert Walker of the LSWR and later the Southern, and Lord Stamp who presided over the LMS during the 1930s looking at every tiny detail through the eyes of a hard economist.

The war years and nationalisation with rule by committee has virtually submerged personalities so that BR managers today are shunted around the system from one region to another, and even with attempts to broaden responsibilities of local management nobody is really sufficiently autonomous to take every decision himself without reference to higher authority or to established policy dictated from elsewhere. Even BR chairmen, with the possible exception of Dr Richard Beeching, have been denied the freedom of their pre-grouping predecessors because of constant Government interference in overall direction of policy and resources. The days of the all-round railway general manager, virtually in command and standing or falling by his own decisions, are over. Or are they?

The expansion during the last two decades of privately run preserved railways in so many parts of the country has brought about a new generation of railway general managers, who, in many cases, at the start of their commercial lives had never thought of a career in railway management, even though they had an interest in railways. With the total number of major

operating private railways in Britain — as distinct from depots with movements confined to yards, siding or short lengths of line — nearing the two dozen mark, because of the part they play in tourism, the administration of preserved lines is achieving an importance undreamed of when the first advertisements appeared for donations to help preserve this or that line 10, 15 and 20 years ago. Indeed running preserved railways today is becoming big business. It is even wrong to call many of them preserved railways for, having been restored, they are again fully active railways in their own right. Some are not even private, for they are administered by public companies, although they are still regarded as private lines to distinguish them from nationalised 'big brother'.

The organisation and financing of the steam tourist railways, for that is really their main function, varies from line to line and much depends on the length of

time they have been in existence. Most started life with appeals for donations from preservation societies formed by railway enthusiasts, for business capital seemed an unlikely source of money for purchase of a line from British Railways, since profit and good return on capital and a steam operated railway did not go hand in hand, or so it seemed.

Most of the early railway preservation schemes took the Talyllyn pioneers as their example and hoped that their ventures would just about cover costs by using as much unpaid volunteer labour as possible and financial resources that did not expect a dividend. Certainly a few of the early schemes, suffering perhaps as much from financial inexperience on the part of their organisers as overkeenness to get trains running, left themselves wide open to exploitation by those more expert in business finance and management, and found that the railway enthusiast members did not quite have the say that had been expected. Equally many railway enthusiasts then, as now, do not have quite that essential grasp of economics in today's conditions and enthusiasm for a project sometimes outweighs the need for a commonsense financial appraisal.

From the start, some railways organised their affairs so that the enthusiast society, as a body perhaps established as a Trust, held the majority of

Below left: *Volunteer cleaners of Black Five No 45110, now named* RAF Biggin Hill, *at Ashford in February 1970, are girls from a Bromley school, grateful for training received for a Duke of Edinburgh Award scheme.*/D. A. Idle

Below: *Restoration work on GWR 5101-class Prairie tank No 4141 at Hampton Loade, Severn Valley Railway, in May 1975.*/David M. Cross

shares of the limited company which actually owned and operated the railway. By this means the shares cannot be sold by individuals so that the controlling interest in the company does not pass out of the hands of the preservation society concerned. Other railways are organised on more conventional business lines, with shareholders owning shares in the normal way so that the railway is financed and run as a commercial business undertaking. Nearly all the railways running daily services through the summer tourist season have a nucleus of permanent paid staff and in the case of those railways running as full commercial undertakings there could be a clash of interest between the use of volunteer labour from a supporting enthusiast body and the basic profit motive of the company. So much depends on the company and its administrators.

In the case of lines with preservation society control, profit is not necessarily the prime aim although clearly there must be adequate excess of income over expenditure to allow for future renewals and heavy repairs. When takings only just cover operating costs, or do not cover them at all then there are problems, for loss-making lines cannot run for long in such circumstances nor are subsidies likely. Moreover, even with voluntary assistance, expenditure on just one major locomotive repair can run into thousands of pounds.

With economic restraints, opposing pressures from enthusiasts, and possibly company shareholders or even directors, the interest in running 'your' railway, and the knowledge that it is making a major contribution as a tourist attraction, the management and operation of today's tourist railways is at one and the same time a major headache and a challenge. The manager of a tourist line — and included in that term are all the designation variations, superintendent of the line, general manager, line manager, managing director, call them what you will, for the title varies from line to line — must know something about everything that makes up a railway. Ideally he should be able to turn his hand to most things, for he might have to stand in for someone who does not turn up for duty in any department, except engine driving, for the Department of Transport railway inspecting officers are quite firm that engine driving must only be done by qualified engine drivers. That does not mean to say that one well-known general manager with long experience of driving could not be seen on the footplate at peak times, while another can be seen as part of the permanent way gang on track maintenance and repair.

The manager is really the link between the board of directors, whether appointed from the controlling preservation society or outside commercial interests, the staff and public. He might or might not have control of engineering matters and some lines have a chief engineer who reports directly to the board. On others the general manager has engineering and commercial assistants who report to him. Usually,

though, the general manager looks after the operating and commercial aspects of the line but must work closely with the engineering side whatever the formal set-up. Thus his responsibilities cover ticket offices, stations, train operation, the sideline attractions such as bookshop and buffet, train catering, supplies and stores, timetables, operating rules and regulations, safety, staff — including the rostering of known volunteers both for operating duties and for special works or maintenance parties — publicity and accounts. He would supervise the arrangements for any special parties of passengers, for example regular coach tours with all their attendant reservations, the running of through BR excursions on to the railway where such is possible, or the operation of special trains in conjunction with BR specials to an

Below left: *Coaching in firing for ex-Olympic sprinter Barrie Kelly on Dart Valley's No 7827* Lydham Manor *during a DVR Association North West Group's promotional occasion.* /DVRA North West Group

Right: *DVR Association members working on the smokebox and boiler tubes of GWR 0-4-2T No 1450 at Ashburton.*/G. Gwilliam

Below: *A Keighley & Worth Valley Railway member working from the firebox on boiler tubes of BR 2-6-4T No 80002 at Haworth.*/R. Higgins

interchange station where gauge differences prevent through running. He might have an assistant to take over some of the workload or assistance from the allied enthusiast society but usually there is no more than a small office staff of perhaps two or three, and then sometimes only for the operating season.

During the season it is often a 12-hour day, seven days a week from probably May to mid-September. Even though the train service does not start until mid-morning the manager is usually on duty at least by 08.30 and perhaps earlier just to keep an eye on preparations for the day's operations. Moreover passengers will start arriving for the first train up to an hour before it leaves so that the station buffet and the souvenir shop are likely to be open well before the first train goes. In any case the manager, or an operating

Left: *Members of the Great Western Society lining out and lettering auto-trailer No 231 in the part of Didcot motive power depot rented by the Society from BR./Great Western Society*

Below left: *Also at the GW Society's Didcot shop, a GWR clerestory third built in the early 1900s undergoing restoration./Nigel Hunt*

Below: *A Dart Valley Railway guard in GWR guard's uniform of the 1930s./Robert Price*

deputy such as the station manager, will be keeping an eye on train preparation and ensuring that staff are organised on filling train toilets with water, that the buffet car is being stocked up and that the coaches have been swept out and cleaned, with door handles polished. Nothing will remind a passenger of the bad old days of the steam age more than grease or soot on his hands from a dirty door handle. As most tourist lines run through highly scenic areas windows must naturally be clean. Reserved accommodation must be checked for any parties that have been arranged, so that seats are kept free until the party arrives. About half an hour or so before departure of the first train the ticket office will start booking and the ticket clerk will need to be on duty at the ticket window.

The locomotive crew will have started their day much earlier probably around 07.00 when the fire will be lit. Some lines might have a man available for engine preparation so that he can get things under way before the engine crew signs on. In that way the enginemen spend their duty time primarily on driving rather than in preparation and disposal of the engine. Much depends on the line and the extent of the train service. On some lines with a fairly intensive service during the day extending into the evening during the peak summer months, it almost needs two shifts to cover all the duties including lighting up in the morning and clearing out the fire, cleaning the tubes and disposing of ash at the end of the day's work.

A line whose service finishes during the late afternoon in contrast, can just get through on a single shift. Usually the fireman will let the fire burn right down on the last trip and the embers are thrown out when the engine has finished for the day since it would not be safe to leave an engine in full steam and with a good fire overnight without a night-duty engineman available to keep an eye on boiler water levels. Normally the boiler is topped up last thing after the day's work and steam pressure gradually falls overnight. In any case the engine is still warm by the morning and it does not take very long to get back to full steam, probably no more than an hour or two depending on the size of engine and the state of the boiler. A large mixed-traffic engine being steamed from cold is another matter and might take up to four hours.

The signalman is one of the most important operating positions on the line and the men undertaking this job must also be fully qualified. They might not necessarily be on the permanent staff, but if volunteer staff they are usually regulars, employed, after training and passing out, on the one job. Sometimes they might be BR men and will be trained already. Essentially, safe operation on the tourist railways is of equal importance to that on BR, and the Department of Transport inspecting officers require high standards, possibly more stringent than on BR because of the non-permanent staff on some jobs. The line manager is responsible for ensuring that safety standards and requirements are maintained. Most, but not all, lines have a maximum speed limit of 25mph which is strictly enforced. One or two have higher speed limits but the conditions of operation are then more stringent in relation to staff, signalling, and maintenance standards.

Usually the line manager will see the signalman (or if more than one, the signalman working the principal box) to check that all is well, and possibly to have a quick run through any special workings which would alter timetables or shunting programmes, or discuss the running of a special train. Nearly all the tourist railways are of single track, which have more regulations than a double line, to prevent any possibility of head-on collisions. Some lines operate a timetable which can be covered by one train, so that normally no problem arises and the line is worked under what are known as one-train operation (OTO) regulations. Movements on to the single line can only be made under the authority of the OTO staff. This is a wooden or metal staff labelled with the station at each end of the section to which it applies. There is only one staff for the section and no train is allowed to travel on the single line unless the driver is in possession of the staff.

In such a case the line is worked as one long single section with probably a manned signalbox at the principal end where the headquarters, engine shed and carriage sidings are located. The signalman controls shunting, and the layout in the station will almost certainly be fully signalled. When the train is ready to leave the signalman will hand the driver the staff for the section and clear the starting signal. When the train reaches the far end the guard will take the staff and using the key on the end of the staff will unlock ground frame point levers to change the points for the engine to run round the train for the return journey. As it approaches the principal station the driver will sound the engine whistle to warn the signalman of its approach — the latter will be expecting it according to the timetable — and he will clear the signal for it to enter the station.

The OTO system has its limitations for only one train can be on the line at one time, and trains must run alternately backwards and forwards over the line. Two trains cannot follow in the same direction (unless the staff is taken back between them by some means, perhaps by a light engine which then couples on the front of the second train). There is a system which uses the train staff in conjunction with tickets which provides more flexibility in single line operation but the railway inspecting officers are more likely to insist on electric staff or key token systems if a line operates more than one train. With this form of operation there are several staffs or tokens for each section, but they are contained in electrically interlocked staff or token block instruments, with one instrument at each end of the section, in such a way that only one token can be released at a time, and that one must be returned to the instrument at either end of the section before another token can be released.

In normal use the electric token system needs a signalman at both ends of a single line section as the action of obtaining a token is co-operative by both men at the same time. This system has been modified for use on some tourist lines to what is known as no-signalman token. With this system, provided that no token has previously been released, the fireman of a train wanting to proceed on to the next single line section ahead operates the token instrument himself and can obtain a token. The train then proceeds

Left: *Coupling locomotive to train on the Festiniog Railway.* /J. R. Barton

Right: *The token is taken at Bewdley for the run to Arley on the Severn Valley Railway.*/Graham F. Scott-Lowe

Above: *On the Talyllyn Railway, interior of the signal ground frame at Pendre.*/T. R. Rimmer

Right: *More-sophisticated control is provided by radio-telephone communication on the Ravenglass & Eskdale Railway.*/Ivor Nicholas

through the section and when reaching the far end of the section the token is put in the instrument there. Until it is put in and the instruments put back in phase a second token cannot be withdrawn for a following train or for one in the opposing direction. The fireman then repeats the action with the instrument for the next section ahead. The token instruments are situated in signalboxes at passing loops. Even if only one train is on the entire line at one time the train crew must repeat the procedure at the instruments at each passing place.

Indeed, although in such circumstances it is technically possible to have an OTO staff interlocked with but over-riding the individual section tokens for long section working, the inspecting officers wanted to standardise the method of operation at all times regardless of the number of trains needed for the timetable. When this system was installed on the Talyllyn Railway some years ago it was stipulated that crossing movements at passing loops by two passenger trains would not be permitted unless a signalman was on duty, even though it would have been quite feasible for the train crews to have signalled themselves through the passing loops and on into the single-line section.

But safety in train operation is only one aspect. Essential in the running of any railway, and particularly a steam railway, is proper maintenance and inspection of locomotive boilers. That staff engaged on boiler work must be fully trained goes

without saying. Often the men looking after locomotives on the tourist lines are former BR fitters who just love steam. Looking after a steam locomotive is heavy, dirty and usually awkward work, for many components are not easily accessible. Moreover some tourist lines do not have the workshop equipment or other facilities that are found in BR works. Several did not even have covered accommodation at the start and have made repair sheds one of their first priorities, for you cannot take an engine to bits out in all weathers. Moreover at some time it will be necessary to lift an engine (and coaches for that matter) to get at springs and suspension, to remove axlebox bearings and, less often, to remove wheels for turning new flange and tread profiles on a wheel lathe. Few lines have the equipment for all this and even if wheels and axles can be removed they usually have to be sent away to a BR or other major works with wheel-turning equipment.

Engine boilers are subject to stringent testing both cold under hydraulic pressure and in steam. Few boilers are anywhere near new but provided the outer plates are sound and not corroded, boiler life, with

Left: *Removing the restricted headshunt for running round at Oxenhope, Keighley & Worth Valley Railway, by adding a length of track in 1971./R. Higgins*

many engines by small teams of absolutely dedicated enthusiasts who have often worked for years against almost impossible odds in restoring locomotives to working order. Every part has been carefully stripped down, cleaned, repaired or rebuilt in an untiring effort to bring steam machinery back to life.

All this really comes within the province of the chief engineer of a line but naturally the line manager likes to know what is going on. Another safety aspect which does come under the manager is that of the public. So many people, particularly railway enthusiasts, have the idea that because a railway is run by enthusiasts they can walk across tracks or take photographs from dangerous vantage points. Nothing could be further from the truth. Trains need to be treated with respect, and passengers and visitors just cannot be allowed the freedom of the line. While all lines carry public liability insurance it is up to the manager to ensure that normal safety precautions are taken and that passengers keep to the platforms and do not wander into danger.

Apart from the prime function of running trains, almost of equal importance are what might be termed the sideline business activities of a tourist railway, usually consisting at least of a buffet and railway sales counter for books and souvenirs. Several railways have first-class shops selling not only books, magazines, railway relics, postcards and stationery, but also a good range of fancy gifts. On some lines restaurant, buffet and shop takings form a good part of the railway's overall revenue, in a few cases as much as 50 per cent. It is not generally realised just how important this additional revenue is to most lines, for even with a large amount of volunteer labour and minimal permanent paid staff, rapidly rising costs, particularly of fuel and oil, and certainly the cost of materials for locomotive and track maintenance, most lines hardly cover their operating costs from passenger fares alone and are dependent on any extra revenue from other activities to provide enough for repairs and servicing and to make a small profit.

Moreover financial results can so easily be affected by the weather. The long fine summer of 1976 might have been just right for beach activities but it did not help tourist railways, which found passenger totals much lower on hot sunny days than on the few dull cloudy days. In contrast some railways have seen the importance of attracting tourists with indoor entertainment to supplement train rides, for example museums of railway relics, or model railways which can provide enough interest to attract visitors for say, an afternoon, and bring valuable additional revenue, especially during bad weather.

limited service on tourist lines, can be prolonged for many more years, but at a cost, by renewing tubes, stays and all the components inside a boiler which can and do corrode or leak from time to time. One of the problems today is that spares are no longer made, at least in quantity. For a few years after the final withdrawal of steam locomotives from BR spares could be obtained by cannibalising other locomotives but this source has dried up. If patching up or repair cannot be done then it means making the part, often specially and at high cost if done commercially.

Through the various associations to which most of the tourist railways belong the maintenance problems of one line are usually shared by several, so that joint orders for new parts can help to cut unit costs. Sometimes one railway in need of a particular part will advertise the fact and find that another railway can spare one from a dozen or so it has in stock. Bartering is not unknown either! There is little doubt that some really first-class restoration work, not merely on the outside which is the least of the worries, but on mechanical parts and boilers, has been carried out on

Fare levels are controversial in themselves, for most of the tourist lines charge rates per mile much higher than BR, despite the use of volunteer labour. But running a steam railway in today's conditions is an expensive business and it costs far more per engine to run a small fleet of four or five than much larger numbers on a national system. Yet there is a limit on the amount by which fares can be raised to cover increases in costs, especially during national economic problems in the country as a whole when families are watching closely the cost of a day's outing. As mentioned earlier the method by which the line is run and financed also play an important part, for commercial profit and steam railways do not always go together today.

Even so, railway enthusiasts occasionally let their eagerness get the better of sound economic management so that unless there is firm control of finances by the manager or managing director and the board, financial disaster can so easily turn into reality. Already several railway preservation schemes which at first sight seemed promising have foundered before getting off the ground, and a few established tourist railways have had financial frights. To have a real chance of steaming into the 1980s all tourist railways, whatever their constitution, must be run as far as possible on normal commercial lines and not only cover costs of operation and maintenance and the employment of essential staff but provide finance for future works on the line and, of prime importance, to the locomotives, for steam engines eventually wear out and need major overhauls.

While several engines in steam might look attractive it is also expensive in fuel and crew costs. Several railways have found, sometimes the hard way, that unless the train service actually needs it, to have more than the bare minimum of power in steam is today totally uneconomic. This is where conflict can arise between enthusiasts and a line's management; those who pay their subscriptions to a society cannot see why the line is not run as they think it should be, and the management has the unenviable task of actually operating it and balancing the books.

Sometimes there are problems in making the best use of volunteer labour. Certainly there are keen

Two major Festiniog Railway construction jobs, a new passing loop (below) and digging out a cutting for the new deviation line./Ron Fisher, Festiniog Railway

enthusiasts who are willing to give up say two weeks' holiday or occasional weekends to work on the line but otherwise live too far away to make regular appearances. The DoT railway inspecting officers, as we have already seen, are firmly against casual volunteers in operating positions, particularly for signalling and engine crew duties. Regular volunteers might get the chance to work as firemen as part of training towards passing out as drivers but the opportunities for such duties for casual volunteers are limited. Certainly we cannot all be engine drivers and someone must do other jobs such as carriage cleaning, sweeping platforms, ticket clerk, ticket inspector, or helping the regular track gangs in keeping vegetation at bay. All this needs careful rostering. Where volunteers can be used whoever keeps the register of volunteers, whether the manager or someone from the preservation society working in close contact with the manager, will need to know well in advance who will be available for duty. A volunteer turning up unannounced is often as much of a nuisance as one expected who does not turn up.

This is why enthusiasts working on tourist lines must accept the organisation and discipline exactly as if they were on the full-time paid staff. Equally it is team spirit that makes these railways such a success and why some of the staff and the manager will work all day and more if needed to make the passengers happy. Out of season there is not the pressure when the trains are not running — although some lines operate a weekend service almost throughout the winter months — but there is still winter maintenance to do and the major jobs which need good co-ordination if they are to go smoothly. Here again preservation society members are often well to the fore but as on BR every detail must be planned in advance with materials and men in the right place at the right time if relaying, bridge repairs, or whatever job is being undertaken will be completed to time.

Although during the winter the line manager can have a slightly easier job, all too soon timetables for the following season must be agreed, publicity leaflets and brochures printed and distributed to hotels, guest houses and local information offices, advertising schedules arranged and estimates obtained from the engineer on locomotive and rolling stock availability. At the end of the financial year someone has to add up all the money received and spent, assess the value of the assets and decide whether the line has made a profit or not. The shareholders, whether preservation society members or outside investors, must be told the results and whether it has all been worth it.

The managers of today's tourist lines have an unenviable job. They have their worries and they work long hours in the season, but I do not think any of them would want it any other way.

Where Live Steam can be Seen

B. K. Cooper

STEAM RAILWAYS

The following notes on the principal lines operating steam trains are for general guidance only. Periods of operation given are approximate and actual dates can be obtained from the railways, most of whom will supply timetables on receipt of a stamped addressed envelope. Timetables of the Welsh lines are published collectively in a folder, *The Great Little Trains of Wales,* produced by the Narrow Gauge Railways of Wales Joint Marketing Panel, c/o Wharf Station, Tywyn, Gwynedd. A leaflet, *Steam Trains in the British Isles,* is published annually by the Association of Railway Preservation Societies.

LONDON AREA AND SOUTH EAST

Romney, Hythe & Dymchurch Light Railway

The 15in-gauge Romney, Hythe & Dymchurch Light Railway is perhaps the best known of the working steam railways to the general public. It celebrated its Golden Jubilee in 1977 and is situated in a popular holiday area close to London and the centres of population of South-East England. The line runs from Hythe, through Dymchurch and New Romney, to Dungeness, 13½ miles. At Dungeness the line doubles back on itself in a loop which allows the running on occasions of non-stop trains from Hythe,

through Dungeness and back to their starting point. A number of intermediate stations and halts are served. The railway was built as a scaled-down version of a main line of its day. This is still its image, although just as main-line railways have changed in their equipment since fifty years ago, so has the RH&DR. A major renovation of signalling and rolling stock has been carried through to meet the expectations of today's public. The railway has about 300,000 visitors a year of whom only a small proportion are railway enthusiasts. But it is managed by railway enthusiasts who strike a balance between preserving the old and maintaining a suitable standard of service and amenities.

All 10 of the original steam locomotives are still to be seen on the railway, this figure including the contractor's engine, *The Bug,* used during the construction of the line and now preserved in the railway's museum. The others comprise seven Pacifics and two 4-8-2s. A further Krupp Pacific has recently been acquired from Germany. A programme of building 20-seat coaches on old but extended underframes was undertaken in 1973. Colour-light signals with modern route-indicating and subsidiary aspects have been installed, but some of the semaphores has been reinstated.

The railway is open daily from Easter to September inclusive. From February to Easter and in October and November trains run between Romney and Hythe at weekends. Timetables giving full details are available from The Manager, Romney, Hythe & Dymchurch Light Railway, New Romney, Kent TN28 8PL (telephone New Romney 2353). East Kent buses connect Hythe Station, RH&DR, with Folkestone Central BR.

Below: Hythe Station on the Romney, Hythe & Dymchurch Railway in August 1969, with 4-6-2 Northern Chief *(1925) entering the station and 4-6-2* Hurricane *(1926) waiting to take its train to Romney./R. E. B. Siviter*

Above: *Headed by 0-6-2T* Conqueror *(1923), Whipsnade &
Umfolozi No 3, a train approaching Whipsnade Central.*
/Mimram Studio

Above right: *KESR Terrier No 10* Sutton, *built 1876, climbing
Tenterden bank with ex-LNWR coach No 101* Woolwich *in the
line's centenary cavalcade in September 1976.*
/Brian Stephenson

Whipsnade & Umfolozi Railway

The 2ft 6in-gauge Whipsnade & Umfolozi Railway
at Whipsnade Zoo runs through the animal paddocks
in a continuous circuit three miles long. Trains are
normally steam-hauled although a diesel may be run
before 13.00. The line has 0-6-2 tanks by Manning
Wardle, Kerr Stuart and Bagnall, and a Kerr Stuart
0-4-2. Trains run daily from the beginning of April
until the end of October. The line is provided primarily
for those who have paid their entrance to the zoo, but
arrangements can be made for parties of 10 or more to
travel without buying tickets to the zoo itself. These
arrangements must be made in advance, and the zoo
authorities notified of the time of arrival so that parties
can be met at the zoo gates and escorted to the
railway. A former South African Railways Class 7
steam locomotive (4-8-0) which was later sold to the
Zambesi Sawmills Railway in Zambia is on view,
together with a Rhodesia Railways balcony-ended
clerestory sleeping car. Both items were presented to
the wildlife artist, David Shepherd, by the Government
of Zambia and brought to this country by him as

depicted in the BBC TV film *Last train to Mulobezi*. It
is intended eventually to transfer the locomotive and
coach to the East Somerset Railway, Cranmore.

The Whipsnade & Umfolozi Railway is operated by
Pleasure Rail Ltd. Arrangements for party travel
should be made through its office at 20 John Street,
London WC1N 2DL.

Kent & East Sussex Railway

Colonel Stephens, the light railway pioneer,
engineered and operated the Kent & East Sussex
Railway to provide communications for the area of
Kent between Robertsbridge on the SER main line to
Hastings, and Headcorn on the same company's boat
train route to Folkestone and Dover. Ten miles of its
standard-gauge track remain between Tenterden and
Bodiam, of which the four miles from Tenterden Town
to Wittersham Road are preserved and worked today
by the Tenterden Railway Co Ltd. Among steam
locomotives working the line are Brighton 'Terrier'
No 10 *Sutton* and Norwegian 2-6-0 No 19. An ex-
Great Western AEC diesel railcar is included in some
train formations. Another vehicle on the line, Pullman
car *Barbara*, is used in 'wine and dine' specials run on
Saturday evenings in summer. The line is open at
weekends and bank holidays from April to October on
Wednesday afternoons from June to August, and daily
during part of August. Outside these periods and on
certain other dates services run on Sundays only.
Details are obtainable from the Commercial Manager,
Kent & East Sussex Railway, Tenterden Town
Station, Tenterden, Kent TN30 6HE (telephone 2943).

Leighton Buzzard Narrow Gauge Railway

The Leighton Buzzard Narrow Gauge Railway works trains over a three-mile section of the 2ft-gauge Leighton Buzzard Light Railway, an industrial line built to carry sand quarried on the outskirts of the town. It is characterised by some 0-4-0 and 0-6-0 locomotives of highly distinctive appearance, among them the vertical-boiler *Chaloner* built in 1877 and now a centenarian. Trains run from Pages Park Station, Billington Road, Leighton Buzzard, to Pages Park on Sundays from the end of April to the end of September and during bank holiday weekends. Details can be obtained by telephoning Pages Park Station, Leighton Buzzard 3888 (telephone answering machine).

The Bluebell Railway

Today's Bluebell Railway keeps alive a portion of the former LBSCR line from East Grinstead to Lewes. Its trains run between Sheffield Park Station, on the A275 road from Lewes to Wych Cross, and Horsted Keynes, where in past years the line was joined by a branch from the Brighton main line at Haywards Heath. Travelling between these points, the passenger in a Bluebell train discovers deep rural Sussex in a way it would be hard to match elsewhere, or by other means of transport. The Bluebell has its LBSCR associations in motive power and rolling stock but by its own efforts and those of other preservation societies working with it now presents an ever-widening panorama of Southern steam, and not only branch line. Among the railway's own 'classics' are the LBSC 'Terrier' *Fenchurch* and an LSWR Adams 4-4-2 tank, while the Bulleid Society operates its West Country Pacific, *Blackmore Vale,* and has undertaken preservation of a Bulleid Q1 0-6-0, more remarkable for its originality than its beauty but a definite landmark in steam locomotive evolution to match an age of austerity and realism.

The Bluebell Railway operates services at weekends throughout the year and during the week in summer. Public transport to its termini is not abundant, but

when major events are being staged there are special bus services from Haywards Heath and through bookings from many Southern Region stations.

There are interesting LBSCR relics in the museum at Sheffield Park. A new bookstall was opened at that station in 1976 and catering facilities are ample for the visitor proposing to spend a day on the line. Enquiries, Newick 2370.

Below left: Leighton Buzzard NGR's 1877 de Winton 0-4-0T Chaloner heading a train towards Pages Park during the locomotive's 100th year in July 1977./Kevin Lane

Below: A Sheffield Park-Horsted Keynes train on the Bluebell line in May 1975 hauled by SECR Class C 0-6-0 No 592 (1902) and LSWR 4-4-2T No 488 (1885)./Brian Morrison

Bottom: Bagnall 0-6-2T approaching Kemsley Down with a train on the Sittingbourne & Kemsley LR in August 1974. /Brian Morrison

Sittingbourne and Kemsley Light Railway

The origin of the present Sittingbourne and Kemsley Light Railway was a 2ft 6in-gauge line built to convey materials and employees for a paper-making company. A two-mile section of this line from Sittingbourne to Kemsley Down is now leased to the Sittingbourne and Kemsley Light Railway Ltd, which operates steam passenger services at weekends and bank holidays from April to October, also mid-week in August and on certain other occasions. The locomotives are narrow-gauge industrials of considerable historic interest to students of the steam railway's part in internal industrial transport.

Sittingbourne SKLR station is in Milton Road, Sittingbourne, close to Sittingbourne BR and the A2 road. There are refreshment rooms there and at Kemsley Down, the latter also having a picnic area, but no road access. Information can be obtained from the Secretary, SKLR, 51 Russell Drive, Whitstable Kent CT5 2RG, or by telephoning Sittingbourne 24899 at weekends and on other operating days.

SOUTHERN AND WESTERN AREAS

East Somerset Railway

BR 2-10-0 No 92203 and 4-6-0 No 75029, now named *Black Prince* and *The Green Knight* respectively, were bought by David Shepherd, the wildlife artist, after he became possessed by the preservation urge while painting scenes in locomotive sheds. They are now housed, with others, at Cranmore Station in Somerset, and there is a prospect of their running one day between there and Shepton Mallet, three miles away. At present there is restricted scope for running in the station area, where a motive power depot has been built in the style of the Victorian railway builders. The East Somerset Railway at Cranmore is open daily except Christmas Day. Steaming takes place on Sundays and bank holidays between late March and the end of October. Cranmore Railway Station (telephone Cranmore 417) is on the A361 Frome road three miles east of Shepton Mallet.

Left: One of the numerous GWR 0-6-0 pannier tank engines, No 6412, at one time on the Dart Valley Railway, seen here in July 1976 with a train at Dunster on the West Somerset Railway./Brian Morrison

Below left: Commemorating the opening of the East Somerset Railway's new motive power depot in June 1975, David Shepherd's BR 2-10-0 No 92203 Black Prince and 4-6-0 75029 The Green Knight prepare to break the tape. /Graham F. Scott-Lowe

Below: Isle of Wight Steam Railway's LSWR 0-4-4T Calbourne, built 1891, shunting stock at Newport in November 1970./John Goss

Isle of Wight Steam Railway

Havenstreet Station, near Ryde, IOW, was once a passing place on the Ryde-Newport line. Today it is the base of the Isle of Wight Steam Railway which runs trains over about two miles of the old track towards Wootton. Among its locomotives are the ex-LBSC 'Terrier' *Newport,* built in 1878, and the ex-LSWR 0-4-4T *Calbourne,* built in 1891. The line operates on Sundays from early May to late September, on bank holiday weekends, and on Thursday afternoons in July and August. Southern Vectis bus service No 3 runs from Ryde Esplanade and Newport to Havenstreet, with a stop outside the station. Inclusive through Awayday tickets are issued at a number of Southern Region stations, also at Portsmouth Harbour and Southsea (Clarence Pier). Enquiries, Wootton Bridge 882204.

West Somerset Railway

Minehead used to be connected with the Great Western main line at Norton Fitzwarren by a 25-mile branch, but this was closed in 1971. The West Somerset Railway Company was formed to restore a service over as much of the branch as possible, with the ultimate aim of working through to Taunton. This was to be a public transport facility as well as a preservation venture, and so it was planned to run diesel railcar services all the year round, with steam trains at holiday seasons. In 1976 trains began running between Minehead and Blue Anchor (3½ miles) on 28 March and were extended to Williton (9¾ miles) by the end of August. In 1977 a mixed service

of steam trains (Minehead-Blue Anchor) and diesel railcars (throughout) was advertised daily from April to October. The company's ex-GWR 0-6-0PT No 6412 featured in Southern Television's railway adventure series, *The Flockton Flyer*, which was filmed on the line, and ran during 1977 in the livery it had carried for that purpose. Bagnall 0-6-0ST *Victor* has also been regularly at work. The diesel trains are formed of BR/Park Royal motor cars and trailers. Other diesel power has been provided on occasions by the Diesel & Electric Groups's Hymek diesel-hydraulic of the class so long associated with Western Region main-line services. Between Minehead and Williton WSR trains call at Dunster, Blue Anchor, Washford and Watchet. At Washford the Somerset and Dorset Museum Trust has its locomotives and rolling stock in store, including ex-S&D 2-8-0 No 53808. A small museum of S&DJR relics is being set up here.

Places of historic interest and scenic beauty abound along the line — a Norman castle at Dunster, sandy beaches at Blue Anchor, Cleeve Abbey near Washford, and the varied activities of a small seaport at Watchet. Williton is the last surviving example of a Bristol & Exeter broad-gauge station.

The headquarters of the West Somerset Railway Co Ltd is The Railway Station, Minehead (telephone Minehead 4996).

Mid-Hants Railway

Beyond the limit of electrification at Alton, a former London & South Western Railway line wandered pleasantly through the heart of Hampshire to join the main Bournemouth and Weymouth route at Winchester Junction. In its day it was used by a number of scheduled through services but in its later years carried mainly local traffic, providing connections for Waterloo at Alton. It also served an important purpose as a diversionary route for main-line trains. None the less, the Alton-Winchester Junction line was scheduled for closure under the Beeching Plan, although strong local opposition succeeded in having a service maintained until 4 February 1973, when the last train ran. The section of about three miles between Alresford and Ropley has been preserved and has been carrying passenger services since 1977, running at weekends and on bank holidays from April to October. The line meanders between cornfields and the watercress beds from which it takes its name of 'Watercress Line'. Alresford, a typical Victorian country station, is the headquarters of the railway, but it is hoped to build a locomotive shed and museum at Ropley. Present motive power includes the Southern Railway N class 2-6-0 No 31874, now named *Aznar Line*. Among locomotives undergoing restoration is the Urie S15 Locomotive Preservation Group's Urie 4-6-0 No 30506. This is the only preserved example of the work of Robert Wallace Urie, Chief Mechanical Engineer of the London & South Western Railway from 1912 to 1922. The group is working on the locomotive at Alresford and hopes to have it in service on the line in 1979.

Alresford Station is on the A31 Guildford-Winchester Road. Inquiries may be addressed to the Mid-Hants Railway Preservation Society Ltd, Alresford Station, Alresford, Hampshire SO2 9JG. The land over which the railway ran between Ropley and Alton has been purchased and the ultimate aim is to re-lay the track on this section. If this is done, steam trains will again be able to run over Medstead summit, 600ft, approached from Alton by two miles at 1 in 60 and followed by a drop of three miles at 1 in 60/80

Left: *SR N Class 2-6-0 No 31874* Aznar Line *on a crew training run on the Mid-Hants Railway.*/Joma Enterprises

Right: *Busy Jubilee Day (7 June 1977) at Buckfastleigh on the Dart Valley line, with Peckett 0-4-0ST (left) on Yard shunting, 0-6-0PT No 1638 (centre) on a train for Totnes Riverside, and GWR 0-4-2TS Nos 1450 and 1420 heading a train of vintage stock for Staverton.*/J. R. Besley

into Ropley Station. It was this 'hump' which earned the route the name 'Over the Alps' in former days.

The Dart Valley and Torbay & Dartmouth Railways

TWO RAILWAYS in South Devon are operated by the Dart Valley Light Railway Ltd. The older of them is the Dart Valley Railway from Buckfastleigh to Totnes, running over a seven-mile stretch of the former Great Western Railway Totnes-Ashburton branch. In 1973 the company started operations between Paignton and Kingswear under the title Torbay Steam Railway, later changed to its present name of Torbay & Dartmouth Railway.

The Buckfastleigh line closely follows the banks of the River Dart through some of the best of Devon's inland scenery and passes through the intermediate station of Staverton Road, where the visitor in one of the company's steam trains might well feel that time has stood still since the days of the Great Western Railway rural branch at the height of its purposeful but tranquil activity. Buckfastleigh Station is an attraction in itself, with museum, picnic area, miniature passenger-carrying railway and circuit for running traction engines. Steam rallies are held here during the summer season. At Totnes trains terminate in the DVR's own Riverside Station. The DVR emphasis is Great Western, but the visitor can ride in a Gresley buffet car or an observation car of the Southern Railway's Devon Belle. Various GWR tank-engine classes provide the motive power. Some of them have been named in recent years, which underlines the fact that the DVR has a personality of its own. Trains run from April to October. Enquiries to Buckfastleigh 2338.

Although Newton Abbot to Kingswear was a branch off the GWR main line, its holiday traffic and through trains from Paddington gave it a main-line atmosphere. This aspect is preserved today on the Torbay & Dartmouth Railway, with 4-6-0s and a Western-class diesel-hydraulic working traffic as well as tank engines. The T&D's Queen's Park Station is immediately adjacent to Paignton BR. As far as Churston the line gives panoramic views over Torbay and soon afterwards the glistening expanse of the Dart estuary comes into view. From the terminus at Kingswear passengers can cross the river by ferry to Dartmouth. The service is operated from mid-April until October. Enquiries to Paignton 555872.

WALES

Welshpool & Llanfair Light Railway

The Welshpool & Llanfair Light Railway is a 2ft 6in-gauge line built in 1903 to connect Llanfair Caereinion with Welshpool on the Cambrian Railways main line. It was never an economic success, but struggled on under various ownerships until closed by British Railways in 1956. Rescued from oblivion and restored by the Welshpool & Llanfair Light Railway Preservation Co Ltd, it was reopened between Llanfair and Castle Caereinion in 1963, and extended to Sylfaen in 1972. A project for extension to Welshpool is currently in hand. The section from Llanfair to Sylfaen at present operating is 5$\frac{1}{3}$ miles in length. There are fine views on the early stages of the journey of the River Banwy which is crossed by a three-span viaduct before the line begins to climb out of the valley and is carried across a deep ravine by the six-arch Brynelin Viaduct. There are wayside stations at Heniarth and Cyfronydd before Castle Caereinion, where there is a passing loop which also enables locomotives of trains terminating there to run round. This is a fine vantage point for a view of the Vale of Meifod, looking back towards Llanfair, with the Berwyns in the distance and even a glimpse of Snowdon, it is said, on clear days. Continuing to Sylfaen, the line climbs to its maximum altitude of 578ft before dropping down through open country to Sylfaen Halt, the present terminus. Accommodation here was once limited, but the preservation company has lengthened the platform, improved access from the road, and laid in a run-round loop.

Originally the line ran to the centre of Welshpool but the traces of its course are almost obliterated now by building development. The proposed extension from Sylfaen would terminate at Raven Square at one end of the town, 13 miles from Llanfair Caereinion.

Trains are still worked by the locomotives *Earl* and *Countess* which were previously in service up to 1956; they are supplemented today by three others which have seen service overseas, by industrial steam designs, and diesels. Passenger trains operate at weekends and bank holidays from Easter until October. Daily services are run in summer holiday months. Llanfair Caereinion Station is about a third of a mile outside the town on the A458 road to Welshpool. At Sylfaen the line is again close to the A458. Enquiries should be made to the General Manager, The Station, Llanfair Caereinion, Welshpool, Powys SY21 0SF, telephone Llanfair Caereinion (0938-82) 441.

Fairbourne Railway

The 15in-gauge Fairbourne Railway connects Fairbourne with the Barmouth ferry, a 2¼-mile run with intermediate halts at Bathing Beach, Golf House and Penrhyn Bridge. Trains are steam hauled by the Pacific *Ernest W. Twining* or one of the 2-4-2s *Katie* and *Sian*. There is a BR station and Crosville bus services at Fairbourne. The operating company is Fairbourne Railway Ltd, Beach Road, Fairbourne, Gwynedd LL38 2EX (telephone Fairbourne 362). Services are run between early April and mid-October.

Vale of Rheidol Light Railway

British Railways still operates a steam-worked line — the 1ft 11½in-gauge Vale of Rheidol Light Railway running for 12 miles from Aberystwyth through the mountains to Devils Bridge. The Vale of Rheidol was opened by a private company in 1902, absorbed by

Cambrian Railways in 1913, and so passed into the ownership first of the Great Western Railway at Grouping in 1923, and then of British Railways in 1948. Trains are worked by 2-6-2 tank engines specially designed for the line. The oldest is No 9 *Prince of Wales*, which was built by Davies & Metcalfe for the opening of the railway in 1902. Nos 7 *Owain Glyndwr* and 8 *Llywelyn* were built by the Great Western Railway at Swindon in 1923. They can each take a train of six coaches and brake van up to Devils Bridge, finishing the run with a continuous climb of four miles at a ruling gradient of 1 in 50.

New coaches were built for the railway by the GWR in 1938. They are designed purely for tourist traffic, an uninterrupted view of the scenery being the primary consideration.

The railway operates on a seasonal basis from early April or Easter to October. At the peak seasonal period in July there are six services each way daily. Between Aberystwyth and Devils Bridge there are seven intermediate stations, at which all trains call as required. Passengers wishing to alight must notify the guard at the previous calling point. Passengers wishing

to join the train at an intermediate station must make a hand signal to the driver. Train services are shown in the BR passenger timetable. Further information can be obtained from the Area Manager, BR, Shrewsbury; the Divisional Manager, Stoke-on-Trent; or from the *Great Little Trains of Wales* timetable folder published by the Narrow Gauge Railways of Wales Joint Marketing Panel, c/o Wharf Station, Tywyn, Gwynedd.

Below left: *Welshpool & Llanfair 0-6-0T No 1* The Earl, *built in 1903, at Castle Caereinion with a Llanfair Caereinion train in July 1969.*/G. F. Gilliam

Right: *Fairbourne Railway's 2-4-2* Katie *with a full train at Fairbourne Station in August 1971.*/R. E. B. Siviter

Below: *Vale of Rheidol's GWR 2-6-2T No 8* Llywelyn *(1923) arriving with a train at Devils Bridge as No 9* Prince of Wales *waits to leave with another.*/J. Reeves

Snowdon Mountain Railway

The rack railway to the summit of Snowdon is a steam-worked line starting from Llanberis. Its seven locomotives are all 0-4-2 tanks built by SLM, Winterthur, at various dates between 1885 and 1923. Gauge is 2ft 7½in and the journey to the summit is 4¾ miles in length. The line is operated by Snowdon Mountain Railway Ltd, Llanberis, Gwynedd (telephone Llanberis 223). Visitors using public transport can use BR's Bangor Station and proceed from there by bus. The operating season is from early April to early October, also most Saturdays and Sundays in July and August, bank holiday weekends, and reduced service according to demand on certain weekends outside these periods.

Talyllyn Railway

When the 2ft 3in-gauge Talyllyn Railway celebrated its centenary in 1965 it had actually received the death sentence in 1950, but had been reprieved, restored, and nursed back to its present healthy life by the pioneer of the railway preservation societies. This was the first railway in the country to be saved by voluntary activity. The original Talyllyn Railway ran from Abergynolwyn to Tywyn, primarily for slate traffic from the Bryn Eglwys quarry although passenger trains were timetabled from the beginning. Beyond Abergynolwyn Station, the line continued for three-quarters of a mile to the foot of a gravity-worked incline which brought slate down from the quarry. Today this 'mineral extension', terminating at the beautiful Nant Gwernol ravine, has been opened for passenger traffic so that trains from Tywyn make a journey of about eight miles. Highlights of the run are the ravine and waterfalls of Dolgoch, with the train emerging suddenly on to a viaduct. Two of the small four-coupled tank engines survive from the earliest days of the line — *Talyllyn* and *Dolgoch*, and share

Above left: *Talyllyn Railway's 0-4-2ST No 4* Edward Thomas, *of 1921 vintage, near Dolgoch with a train from Towyn in the early years of the railway's reopening.*/R. E. Vincent

Right: *Hunslet 0-4-0ST* Elidir, *a veteran of 1889, with a Penllyn train at Gilfach Ddu on the Llanberis Lake Railway in April 1975.*/R. E. Ruffell

Above: *One of Snowdon Mountain Railway's seven Swiss-built SLM 0-4-2Ts all built between 1895 and 1923, approaching the summit.*/A. R. Prince

Above right: *Festiniog Railway's 1917 American-built 2-6-2T* Mountaineer *at Porthmadog with a Dduallt train in July 1969.* /G. F. Gillham

duties with their juniors, *Sir Haydn* and *Edward Thomas,* built in 1878 and 1921 respectively. There are also some later steam and industrial diesels in the stock.

Tywyn is served by BR and by Crosville buses. The Talyllyn has two stations in Tywyn, Tywyn Wharf (near the BR station) and Pendre, and there are wayside stations at Rhydyronen, Brynglas and Dolgoch en route to Abergynolwyn and Nant Gwernol. Trains run daily from April to September, and daily except Mondays and Fridays in October. Details from Talyllyn Railway, Wharf Station, Gwynedd (telephone Tywyn 710472).

The Festiniog Railway

In 1936 the Festiniog Railway celebrated its centenary. Built to carry slate from the quarries at Blaenau Ffestiniog to the little harbour of Porthmadog for shipment, this 1ft 11½in-gauge line prospered until Blaenau Ffestiniog was linked with the main-line railway system. Then there was a decline in traffic, not compensated for by growing tourist business, and the last passenger train ran in September 1939. There were a few slate trains during the war, but in 1946 the

company ceased operations. The line was restored and reopened at the Porthmadog end by the present Festiniog Railway Company in 1954. Gradually the line was brought back into use as far as Dduallt, but beyond there the course of the old line was blocked by the new reservoir for the Ffestiniog pumped-storage power station scheme and actually diappeared beneath its waters. But the company was still determined to reach Blaenau Ffestiniog and undertook the massive task of building a deviation with a new tunnel. Breakthrough came in 1977 and the trains began running through the tunnel to a terminus at Llyn Ystradau. Starting in coastal surroundings as the train runs along the sea wall, or Cob, at Porthmadog, the journey on the Festiniog Railway takes the passenger into splendid mountain scenery. At Dduallt the train negotiates a spiral which lifts the track by about 35ft in a huge circle of 3500ft. Two of the double-ended articulated Fairlie locomotives for which the Festiniog Railway has long been well-known are still in use on the line.

There is access to the line by BR services at Porthmadog and Minffordd. Crosville buses serve Porthmadog, Minffordd and Tan-y-bwlch. Festiniog Railway trains run daily between April and early November, otherwise at weekends. Details from Festiniog Railway, Porthmadog, Gwynedd (telephone 2384).

Bala Lake Railway

The Bala Lake Railway was opened in 1972 as a tourist line along three miles of the trackbed of a former GWR branch. Built to 1ft 11½in gauge, it connects Bala with Llanuwchllyn and is building up traffic from residents along the lakeside in addition to holiday visitors. Steam power is provided by Hunslet industrial 0-4-0 tank engines, but diesel traction plays an important part, notably a Severn-Lamb Bo-Bo unit. To reach Llanuwchllyn Station turn off the A494 road where signposted five miles south-west of Bala. The station is half a mile past the village and is the headquarters of the line, telephone Llanuwchllyn 666. The line is open daily from Easter to the end of September, then at weekends during October.

Llanberis Lake Railway

Four former Dinorwic slate quarry 0-4-0 steam locomotives are assisted by small industrial diesels in working this 1ft 11½in-gauge line laid along two miles of the trackbed of the former Padarn Railway. The route skirts the lake, giving fine views of the Snowdon range as a background. Trains run non-stop from Llanberis (Gilfach Ddu) to Penllyn (where passengers may not alight), then call at Cei Llydan Halt on the return journey, where there is a picnic area. Operating season is from late May to mid-September. Information from Llanberis Lake Railway, Padarn Park (Gilfach Ddu), Llanberis, Gwynedd (telephone 549). By road, turn off A4068 opposite Snowdon Mountain Railway entrance.

EAST MIDLANDS AND EAST ANGLIA

Nene Valley Railway

Among the plans of the Peterborough Development Corporation for expanding the City of Peterborough was the creation of Nene Park along the valley of the River Nene from the city centre towards Wansford. There lay the disused track of the Peterborough-Northampton line, closed finally by BR in 1972. In that year the Peterborough Railway Society was formed. The development Corporation was alive to the possibilities of a preserved railway as one of the attractions in its new park and fruitful collaboration developed between it and the society. As a result the corporation bought the track and leased it to the society to operate as a steam railway between termini at Wansford and Orton Mere, just off Nene Parkway, Peterborough. Wansford Station is the headquarters of the line and a steam centre. It is situated next to the A1 road in the village of Stibbington. Two intermediate stations are planned on the route between Wansford and Orton Mere.

In reconditioning this five-mile line the opportunity was taken to conform to the Berne loading gauge and so allow the running of Continental locomotives. The society had originally been formed to care for a BR standard Class 5 locomotive, No 73050, *City of Peterborough,* but locomotives from the Continent have been bought by individuals and groups, and are now running through Nene Park with trains of varying composition, the most notable perhaps being a Southern Railway 4COR electric set surviving from the stock built for the Portsmouth electrifications of 1937 and 1938.

The railway began public services in 1977, operating on summer Saturdays and Sundays, throughout the Spring and August bank holiday weekends, and on certain Thursdays in June and July. Full details of train services can be had by telephoning Stamford 782021. Buses from Peterborough bus station run to both Orton Mere and Wansford.

North Norfolk Railway

Three miles of the former Midland & Great Northern Joint Railway between Sheringham and Weybourne are operated by the North Norfolk Railway Company. Steam-hauled passenger trains run on Saturdays and Sundays between May and October, and at bank holiday periods. Details from the North Norfolk Railway, Sheringham Station, Sheringham, Norfolk NR26 8RA. Traffic is usually worked by industrial steam tank engines but an LNER B12-class 4-6-0 and GER 0-6-0 No 564 are preserved at Sheringham.

Below: *Inaugural train on the Nene Valley Railway, headed by French Nord 4-6-0 No 3.628 (1911) and Swedish 2-6-2T No 1178 (1914) breaking the tape on 1 June 1977.* /Peterborough Standard

Main Line Steam Trust

Five miles of the former Great Central Railway main line between Loughborough and Rothley in Leicestershire still carry steam trains. By 1969 virtually all the London main line of the GCR had been closed. The Main Line Steam Trust was formed in 1971 to preserve a section running south from Loughborough, and in 1976 the trust formed a company, Great Central Railway (1976) Ltd, to raise money by a share issue to buy what could be saved before the track was lifted. It was successful in purchasing the 5½ miles from Loughborough Central Station to Rothley. The Main Line Steam Trust, with

Below left: Peckett 0-6-0ST arriving at Weybourne, North Norfolk Railway, in August 1976./John R. Smith

Above: A Main Line Steam Trust Loughborough-Rothley & Quorn train headed by Littleton Colliery No 5 (1922) and ex-Norwegian State Railway 2-6-0 King Haakon 7 (1907) in May 1977./John Scrace

its 1800 members, provides the voluntary labour and expertise to run the line. One can ride in main-line stock over a genuine former main line, and for many visitors every mile still brings back memories of journeys in the fast buffet car trains which once ran between Marylebone Station in London, the Midlands and North. The line owns a Gresley buffet car and a first-class restaurant car. Refreshments are seved on all normal services and on certain trains full restaurant car facilities are available. On the run to Rothley, trains call at Quorn & Woodhouse, where there is a car park. Nearing Rothley the line is carried on a viaduct across one end of Swithland Reservoir. All three stations are typical of those on the Great Central's London Extension and the country traversed has the quiet and spacious charm of the English Shires.

The railway's headquarters at Loughborough includes a small relics museum and a station buffet. Loughborough is the home of the ex-Great Central Railway Director class 4-4-0 locomotive No 506 *Butler-Henderson,* on loan from the National Railway Museum. The company's own motive power for working trains is varied, including a Stanier Black Five 4-6-0, a Norwegian Railways 2-6-0, and several industrial tank engines.

Trains run on Saturdays and Sundays throughout the year. Loughborough Central Station is close to the centre of Loughborough and can be reached by BR services to Loughborough LMR from London St Pancras, Nottingham, Sheffield, etc. Enquiries to Loughborough 216433.

69

WEST MIDLANDS

Severn Valley Railway

With a journey of 12½ miles from Bridgnorth to Bewdley, the Severn Valley Railway offers about 50 minutes of steam-hauled travel to the visitor, punctuated by three scheduled stops and 'on-demand' calls at two other stations. The original Severn Valley Railway was 40 miles in length, running from Shrewsbury to Hartlebury with a spur from Bewdley to Kidderminster. Today the SVR Bridgnorth-Bewdley service is extended to Foley Park on this spur on certain occasions, passing the West Midlands Safari Park en route. The spur connects at Kidderminster with BR, enabling through excursions to be run. The railway has a stock of over 30 steam locomotives, some of them of LNER, LMS and GWR origin as well as several built in BR days. Its rolling stock is sufficient to form complete trains in GWR, LMS and BR (carmine and cream) colours. Collections of locomotives and rolling stock are on view at both Bridgnorth and Bewdley.

The railway closely follows the River Severn, and between Arley and Bewdley crosses it by the Victoria Bridge, a 200ft single-span structure high above the river, affording excellent views. Before reaching Bewdley the line skirts Trimpley reservoirs where in summer there is much colourful activity of sailing dinghies. Pleasant country scenery throughout, with

engineering features such as Oldbury Viaduct, Knowlesands Tunnel and the Victoria Bridge to add interest of another kind, combine to make a ride on the Severn Valley Railway an enjoyable experience for every passenger. Here the atmosphere of the steam-worked secondary line lives on as many remember it.

Access to the railway by public transport is convenient. Bus services run to Bridgnorth from Wolverhampton, Stourbridge, Wellington and Shrewsbury; and to Bewdley from Birmingham, Kidderminster and Ludlow. The railway is open at weekends from March to October and daily from late July until early September. Details can be obtained from the General Manager, The Railway Station, Bewdley, Worcestershire DY12 1BG (telephone Bewdley 403816).

Left: LMS 8F No 8233 at Bridgnorth, SVR, in April 1977 ready to start a busy day./Dave Rodgers

Below left: A Chasewater Railway train headed by Hawthorne Leslie 0-4-0ST Asbestos./Railway Preservation Society

Below: Manning Wardle 0-6-0ST No 1317 of 1895, and LMS coach forming a Foxfield Light Railway train in 1970. /D. R. Dankin

Chasewater Light Railway

Track remaining from two former lines in Staffordshire was leased by the Railway Preservation Society in 1965, which licensed the Chasewater Light Railway Co Ltd to run a service. The railway is in Chasewater Pleasure Park, near Brownhills, Staffs, entrance in Pool Road, off the A5 Cannock-Tamworth road near the junction with A452. Locomotives, mainly industrial four-coupled and six-coupled tank engines, are steamed on the second and fourth Sundays of each month from April to September. There are facilities for groups to hire a steam locomotive with brakevan or coach for trips. Eventually it is hoped to run vintage steam trains over an interesting two-mile route in the park. Telephone number for enquiries, 021-523 8516.

Foxfield Light Railway

Foxfield Colliery, near Cheadle, is now occupied by Tean Minerals Ltd, which owns the four-mile standard gauge line built to connect the colliery with the North Staffordshire Railway near Blythe Bridge, Staffs. Today the line is operated with the owner's permission by the Foxfield Light Railway Society Ltd with steam motive power appropriate to its industrial past. Trains run on Sundays from April to October and on bank holidays, providing a trip in an environment which makes interesting changes en route between the industrial and the scenic, with the 13th century Caverswall Castle coming into view at one point and a glimpse of 17th century Stansmore Hall. At Blythe Bridge trains terminate in a fan of sidings. Potteries Motor Traction bus service 86B operates in conjunction with the trains on Sundays from Longton or Cheadle, with inclusive rail/bus tickets. The bus stop at Godley Brook is about 200yd from the station. By road, turn left at Blythe Bridge off the A50 Stoke-Uttoxeter Road. Enquiries, phone Uttoxeter 4669.

NORTH-WEST ENGLAND

Lakeside & Haverthwaite Railway

In 1869 the Furness Railway extended its branch from Ulverston beyond Newby Bridge to Lake Windermere, where Lakeside Station gave cross-platform access to the steamers. Passenger traffic was withdrawn in 1965 and goods trains ceased to run after 24 April 1967. Road construction later severed the line south of Haverthwaite and today the 3½ miles from Haverthwaite to Lakeside are isolated, but still running as a steam railway. Here two LMS Fairburn 2-6-4Ts and a Stanier Black Five are still at work alongside various steam and diesel industrials. Trains from Haverthwaite climb steeply for three-quarters of a mile, after which slightly easier gradients follow to the summit at Newby Bridge Halt. From there the line dips gently to Lakeside. Throughout the journey the line closely follows the west bank of the River Leven, passing through meadows, woodland, rock cuttings and a tunnel. For three-quarters of a mile out of Lakeside the line is bordered by tall trees, with the river literally a stone's throw from the carriage window.

Trains run daily from mid-May to the end of October, connecting with Lake Windermere steamers from Bowness. Haverthwaite Station, headquarters of the railway (telephone Newby Bridge 594), is on the A590 Barrow trunk road.

Ravenglass & Eskdale Railway

Twice in a hundred years the Ravenglass & Eskdale Railway has been saved from extinction. The first occasion was when the original 3ft-gauge line from Boot to Ravenglass, built to carry iron ore to the Furness Railway, was converted to 15in gauge as primarily a passenger-carrying tourist line early in the first world war. At that time the inland terminal was brought back from Boot to Beckfoot; later it was changed to a new station at Dalegarth as at present. The fortunes of the line varied after the second world war and it was put up for sale in 1958 and 1959 without a purchaser being found. In 1960 it was to be auctioned, in lots if necessary, but it was in fact purchased in its entirety by local enterprise supported by a preservation society. Today the seven-mile line through Miterdale and Eskdale into the mountains of Cumbria is a firmly established attraction for visitors, operating services in summer and winter. Recently its well-known 2-8-2 *River Mite* and 0-8-2 *River Irt* were joined by a new 2-6-2 locomotive *Northern Rock*. In the Jubilee year, 1977, a fast diesel train was introduced and a system of train control by radio telephone was installed to help in dealing with the demands of increasing traffic.

Ravenglass RER station is adjacent to Ravenglass

Above: *LMS Fairburn 2-6-4T in Caledonian blue livery working a Lakeside & Haverthwaite train in August 1973.*/R. E. B. Siviter

Above right: *Ravenglass & Eskdale's 2-8-2T No 8* River Esk, *which ran for a few years with a powered tender as articulated 2-8-2-0-8-0, hauling a full load.*/Neil Dormand

Right: *One of the Isle of Man's 11 Beyer Peacock 2-4-0Ts No 4* Loch, *built 1874, on a Douglas/Port Erin train in June 1974.*/Tim Stephens

BR. Cumberland Motor Services Buses serve Ravenglass and Muncaster Mill, the first station out of Ravenglass. Other intermediate stations are at Irton Road, Eskdale Green, and Beckfoot. There is a picnic area at Dalegarth. Headquarters of the railway are at Ravenglass Station, Ravenglass, Cumbria. Telephone Ravenglass 226. The station is situated off the Barrow to Whitehaven Road, A595.

Isle of Man Railway

The Isle of Man Railway Company operates trains with steam power on about eight miles of the island's former south line between Douglas and Port Erin. Services are basically four trains a day on Sundays to Fridays from mid-May to mid-September. The railway has a fleet of 11 Beyer Peacock 2-4-0 tank locomotives built for the island train services at various dates between 1873 and 1910. Enquiries may be addressed to the Isle of Man Railway Company, PO Box 30, Station Buildings, Douglas, Isle of Man (telephone Douglas 4646).

NORTH-EAST ENGLAND

Middleton Railway

The Middleton Railway, Leeds, saw the first successful use of steam engines in 1812 and was the first standard-gauge railway to be taken over by a preservation society in 1960. Today approximately two miles of track are operated by the Middleton Railway Trust, which has a selection of industrial locomotives and stock appropriate to the character of the line. Some freight traffic is worked commercially, but visitors are carried over a one-mile section between Tunstall Road Halt and Middleton Park Gates, riding in goods wagons. They can join the trains at either point. Tunstall Road Halt can be reached by car from the south by turning off the M1 exit 45 (Beeston, Hunslet), turning right along Tunstall Road and then right again at the roundabout. The line is open from 14.00 at weekends and bank holidays from early April until the end of October. All enquiries should be addressed to Middleton Railway Trust Ltd, Garnet Road, Leeds LS11 5JY, enclosing sae.

North Yorkshire Moors Railway

The North Yorkshire Moors line is one of the most photographed of the preserved lines, probably because of the magnificent spectacle presented by six- and eight-coupled main-line locomotives climbing from its northern terminus at Grosmont up an average gradient of 1 in 49 to Goathland. From there to Pickering the line is diesel-worked for this section passes through the North Yorkshire Moors National Park and the diesels minimise fire risk. The distance from Grosmont to Pickering is 18 miles. Three locomotives owned by the North Eastern Locomotive Preservation Group are based on the line; 0-8-0 No 2238 and 0-6-0 No 2392 of the former North Eastern Railway and LNER K1 class 2-6-0 No 2005. The group also has in its care a Lambton Railway 0-6-2T and ex-LMS Black Five No 4767 *George Stephenson*. For its diesel services the railway operates two Gloucester two-car sets and an AC railbus. A Class 24 diesel locomotive was hired to reduce fire risk at the height of the drought in 1976.

The railway connects with BR at Grosmont, which is served by trains from Darlington, Newcastle and Middlesbrough. United bus services run from York and Scarborough to Pickering, and from Whitby to Goathland and Pickering. There are car parks at Grosmont and Pickering. The railway is open most days from Easter to the end of October. Details of train services can be obtained from North Yorkshire Moors Railway, Trust Office, Pickering Station (telephone 72508).

Worth Valley Railway

The name Keighley & Worth Valley Railway dates back to 1862 when an Act was passed for a branch line from the Midland Railway at Keighley, on the main line from Leeds to Carlisle, to Oxenhope, following the valley which cuts through the surrounding moorland. In its five-mile run the branch leaves the brisk industrial surroundings of Keighley to climb into an area of hills and moors in which the stations of Damems, Oakworth, and Haworth are situated. The last-named is internationally known as the home of the Bronte sisters and the little town is a tourist centre for that reason. A little over a mile further on the railway reaches its terminus on the northern outskirts of the village of Oxenhope. It is a ride of great scenic beauty, with two tunnels and a viaduct to remind the traveller that its construction was quite a formidable undertaking for the original promoters of the branch. From its opening on 13 April 1867 the branch was worked by the Midland Railway. The last British Railways train ran over it in 1962, one hundred years after the Act authorising the line had

Below: Hawthorne Leslie 0-4-0ST working a train on the Middleton Railway in August 1974./Nigel Hunt

Right: LMS Stanier 2-8-0 No 8431 and WD 2-8-0 No 1931 just getting a seven-coach train away from Oakworth towards Haworth, KWVR, with assistance from behind./David Eatwell

Below right: NER Q6 0-8-0 No 3395, of 1918 vintage, with a Grosmont-Goathland train on a North Yorkshire Moors Railway open day in August 1970./L. A. Nixon

been passed. Only six years later it was reopened by the efforts of a preservation society and an operating company.

Keighley & Worth Valley (usually now shortened to Worth Valley) trains today start from a bay platform at Keighley Station, which is easy of access both by rail and bus. The whole area, and particularly Haworth, is well served by public transport. Some impressive main-line locomotives can often be seen at work, for the line has steep gradients. One of the mainstays of the passenger service is an ex-LMS Stanier Class 8F 2-8-0. Motive power and rolling stock can also be viewed in the station yard at Haworth and in a display shed at Oxenhope.

The railway is open most weekends and daily during July and August. Details can be had from the Worth Valley Railway, Haworth Station, Keighley (telephone Haworth 43629).

STEAM CENTRES

In addition to the operating railways mentioned in the preceding pages, there are a number of steam centres in different parts of the country where locomotives are preserved and can often be seen in steam. Usually they operate on short sections of track and rides are given in rolling stock of various types. Particulars of some of the larger centres are as follows.

South-East area

Quainton Road: At this former Metropolitan & Great Central station, north of Aylesbury, the Quainton Railway Society maintains a varied collection of engines and rolling stock in the sidings on both sides of the main line. Open days with engines in steam are held from April to October, but the collection can be visited any weekend. There is a bus from Aylesbury BR station.

Didcot: The Didcot Railway Centre of the Great Western Society occupies the former locomotive depot and yard, in the triangle formed by the WR main line to Bristol and the line to Oxford and the Midlands. Access is gained through the subway under Didcot Station. The centre houses the largest single collection of Great Western Railway locomotives and rolling stock, and includes examples of most GWR main line locomotives which survived to the end of steam. The stock of around 20 locomotives includes Castle, Hall and Manor class 4-6-0s as well as 2-8-0, 2-6-0 and various tank types. The GWS vintage train, formed entirely of restored GWR coaches, has operated on steam hauled specials from Didcot over BR lines, but

the depot also contains its own short demonstration line. Plans for expansion at Didcot include the provision of a second demonstration line, and the re-erection at the centre of various GWR buildings including a typical halt and a timber goods shed. The centre is open on Bank Holiday weekends and two weekends per month from April to October. Refreshments and souvenirs are available and a picnic area overlooks the running line.

Essex

Chappel & Wakes Colne: The collection of the

Stour Valley Railway Preservation Society at Chappel & Wakes Colne Station, off the A604 Colchester-Haverhill road, includes LNER N7 0-6-2T No 69621, which as GER No 999 was the last GER locomotive built at Stratford Works. Another main-line locomotive at the centre is BR 2-6-4T No 80151, which is undergoing restoration. There is also a selection of steam industrials. Steamings are held at intervals from March to October, beginning at 11.00.

Norfolk

Bressingham Steam Museum: The Bressingham collection is housed in the 450-acre nursery surrounding Bressingham Hall, Norfolk. There is a 500yd standard-gauge demonstration line and short 9½in- and 15in-gauge lines. The strength of the collection is in its main-line steam locomotives. Here can be seen Britannia Pacific No 70013 *Oliver Cromwell*, Stanier Pacific No 6233 *Duchess of Sutherland*, LMS 4-6-0 No 6100 *Royal Scot*, and 'Tilbury Tank' No 80 *Thundersley*. Bressingham is two miles west of Diss on the A1066 road. The museum is open on Sundays from May to September, Thursdays from late May to early September, Wednesdays in August, and certain other dates. Telephone, Diss 88386.

Above left: *LSWR Beattie 2-4-0WT, originally built in 1874 by Beyer Peacock but much rebuilt and in service until 1962, running trips at Quainton Road in May 1977, again bearing its LSWR number 0314./John Scrace*

Below left: *One of the 75 WD Austerity 0-6-0STs bought by the LNER as Class J94, No 68067 at work at Chappel & Wakes Colne in April 1974./G. D. King*

Below: *Birmingham Railway Museum's (Tyseley) LMS Jubilee 4-6-0 No 45593* Kolhapur *heading a rail tour special near Chinley in April 1967./Brian Stephenson*

East Midlands

Butterley: The Midland Railway Trust's project aims to portray the history of the Midland Railway by means of a static museum and a working line. The main amenities will be centred on Swanwick, which will form the junction of two short branch lines. The collection of locomotives at the centre includes LMS Class 3F 0-6-0T No 16440 and Class 4F 0-6-0 No 44027, both of which are fully restored, and Pacific No 6203 *Princess Margaret Rose,* which is a static exhibit. Two fine examples of Midland Railway locomotives are on loan from the National Railway Museum, York. These are 2-4-0 No 158A, built in 1866 and the famous 'Spinner' 4-2-2 No 673. The centre is open to visitors at weekends, and information may be obtained from the Midland Railway Trust Ltd, 6 Downing Road, Sheffield S8 7SH.

West Midlands

Birmingham: Birmingham Railway Museum, Warwick Road, Tyseley. The Standard Gauge Steam Trust operates this centre, which is one of the terminal points for main line steam running over BR lines. The collection is notable in having four GWR Castle class 4-6-0s, including double and single chimney versions in the form of No 7029 *Clun Castle* and No 7027 *Thornbury Castle* respectively. LMS Jubilee No 5593 *Kolhapur* is housed at the centre, along with several 0-6-0 tank engines. The depot is open to visitors on Sunday afternoons, except bank holidays. Special open days are announced in advance.

Herefordshire

Hereford: Bulmer Railway Centre, Whitecross Road, Hereford. The centre houses GWR 4-6-0 No 6000 *King George V*, and the Pullmans of the

Bulmers Cider train, plus two industrial diesels; also the Merchant Navy Locomotive Preservation Society's Bulleid Pacific No 35028 *Clan Line* and locomotives of the Worcester Locomotive Society. The centre is ½ mile from Hereford city centre on the A438 Brecon Road. It is open for static display from early April until late September and steamings are held on the third Sunday in each month and certain other days as announced.

Avon

Bristol/Bath: Bitton Railway Centre, on the A431 Bristol-Bath road, has been established by the Bristol Suburban Railway Society on the site of the former Bitton Station on the Midland line from Mangotsfield to Bath. Here the Society preserves and restores locomotives and rolling stock. Rides are given on steam days with Avonside or Hunslet industrial 0-6-0 tank engines as motive power at present, but LMS Stanier Class 5 No 5379 is undergoing restoration. The station is open most weekends and steam days are held at intervals throughout the year.

Derbyshire

Dinting: The Dinting Railway Centre, Dinting Lane, Glossop. This former Great Central Railway steam shed houses a small collection of locomotives and is also host to 'Steam on BR' excursions. LMS 4-6-0s Nos 5596 *Bahamas* and 6115 *Scots Guardsman* are the two most notable locomotives here. Steaming Sundays are held from March to October and on other days during bank holiday weekends. The centre is a mile from Glossop on the A57 Manchester road and is served by buses No 236 or 125 from Manchester. Enquiries can be made by telephone to Glossop 5596.

Lancashire

Steamtown Railway Museum, Carnforth: A noteworthy collection of large locomotives, including the classic Pacific No 4472 *Flying Scotsman* and French and German locomotives is contained in the former Carnforth mpd in Warton Road, Carnforth. Locomotives are steamed frequently, giving the opportunity for rides, the site being about a mile long from end to end. Steamtown is open daily throughout the year from 09.00 to 18.00. Steaming takes place on Sundays from March to October.

SCOTLAND

Falkirk: The Scottish Railway Preservation Society has a depot in Springfield Yard, Falkirk, (near Falkirk Grahamston Station). Two engines from pre-Grouping Scottish railways are preserved here — Caledonian 0-4-4 tank No 419 (built 1907) and NBR 0-6-0 No 673 *Maude* (built 1891) together with various industrials of Scottish interest. The depot is open to the public on most Saturdays and Sundays between 11.00 and 16.00. The society can make up a train of five preserved Scottish coaches from its collection, all able to run in excursion trains on BR.

IRELAND

Whitehead: The Railway Preservation Society of Ireland keeps its stock of historic Irish steam locomotives and vehicles at Whitehead Excursion Station, Co Antrim. Steam excursions over the Irish railway system take place frequently, among them the Portrush Flyer trains in summer. Steam train rides are given at Whitehead on Sunday afternoons in July and August.

Below: *LMS Jubilee and Royal Scot 4-6-0s No 5596* Bahamas *and 46115* Scots Guardsman *at Dinting in May 1970.*
/N. E. Preedy

Index